the LCP Primary Science Dictionary

Sue Fallon & John Butterworth

How to use this dictionary

When you look up a word in this dictionary, you will sometimes find another word in the definition that is printed in **bold** type. You can also look up this word to find out more information about your chosen topic.

Design and illustrations
Lee Nicholls
Design
Simon Dainty • Antony Dickens

Commissioning editor
Halina Boniszewska
Editorial
Nicky Barrett • Halina Boniszewska
Anne Furze • Ellen Holgate

The authors and publisher would like to thank Elizabeth Hooper and
Jill Horswill of St Augustine's School, Kenilworth, for their contribution.

© *LCP* Ltd. First published 2002. Reprinted 2003.
LCP Hampton House • Longfield Road • Leamington Spa • Warwickshire CV31 1XB
Tel: 01926 886914 • **Fax:** 01926 887136 • **Isdn:** 01926 316600
e-mail: mail@lcpuk.co.uk • **website:** www.lcpuk.co.uk

ISBN 1 904178 04 9

Scheme of Work • linked • QCA

A

abdomen noun

In humans and larger animals the middle, front part of the body which contains the stomach and intestines is called the abdomen. In **insects** the back section of the body is called the abdomen.

abdomen

absorbent adjective

Absorbent **materials** (for example toilet paper, sponge) soak up water and many other liquids. Absorbent materials have tiny pockets of air in them which allow the water to be absorbed.

absorb verb to soak up.

absorbency noun This is the word for the property of being able to soak up liquids.

accelerate verb

When an object accelerates it moves faster. In science acceleration means a change of speed or direction. Forces such as pushes and pulls are needed to make an object accelerate.

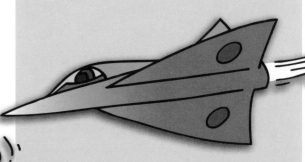

acid noun

Acids are chemical substances with a sharp, sour taste. Vinegar contains acetic acid and lemon juice contains citric acid. Strong acids can burn the skin and eat into metals and rocks.

Some blue vegetable dyes become red when acid is added to them: the redder the vegetable dye becomes, the stronger the acid is. One way of testing whether a **solution** contains acid is to add it to indicator paper (a special paper that has been treated with chemicals), for example litmus paper or universal indicator paper. Acid turns blue litmus paper and universal indicator red.

See also: **alkali**.

acid rain · noun

Acid rain is formed when rain becomes mixed with some waste gases from factories and car engines. Acid rain can kill plants and animals and **erode** (eat away at) the stonework of buildings.

adapt · verb

Species of living things change over very long periods of time, to suit them to life in their surroundings. This process is called **adaptation** (**noun**).

For example, camels have **adapted** to desert conditions.

additive · noun

Materials added to food to preserve it or give it more flavour are called additives.

adolescence · noun

The stage in the **life cycle** between being a child and being an adult.

adolescent noun An adolescent is a young person during the time of adolescence.

adrenaline · noun

Adrenaline is one of the substances called **hormones** that are produced by the bodies of humans and other animals. Adrenaline is produced when someone is frightened, angry, or excited; its effect is a sudden rush of strength and energy.

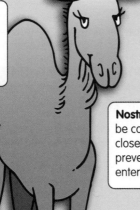

Hump of fat stored on back to give nourishment and water in times of shortage.

Long eyelashes to keep sand out of eyes.

Nostrils that can be completely closed to prevent sand entering them.

Very broad cloven hooves to prevent the camel from sinking into desert sand.

This'll get his adrenaline going!

A

aerodynamic — adjective

An object designed to travel smoothly and easily through air is described as aerodynamic.

agriculture — noun

This is another word for farming.

Many large farms use chemicals and advanced technology to produce more and more crops as cheaply as possible. At the same time some farmers are returning to older **organic** methods of agriculture.

Combine harvester off-loading grain to a tractor.

air — noun

Air is the mixture of gases which we breathe, and which surrounds the Earth to form the **atmosphere**.

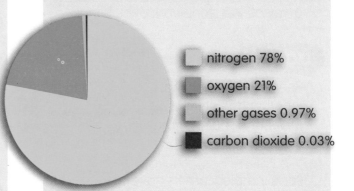

nitrogen 78%

oxygen 21%

other gases 0.97%

carbon dioxide 0.03%

Pie chart showing the proportions of gases that make up air.

air resistance — noun

When an object travels or falls through air, it meets with a force, which **resists** it, or tries to slow it down. This force is called air resistance. The faster the object goes, the greater the resistance.

Air resistance is a kind of **friction** between the object and the invisible particles of air. A similar, but much stronger, resistance is felt in water.

Air resistance can be reduced by making objects streamlined or **aerodynamic**. It can be increased by making objects larger or more spread out. A parachute works because the large open canopy experiences a lot of air resistance.

See also: **water resistance**.

canopy

air resistance

downward pull

because the blood vessels of the retina inside the eye can be seen.

An albino rat or rabbit has pure white fur and pink eyes.

alcohol noun

Alcohol is a colourless liquid that is made when sugar is **fermented** (through the action of a substance called **yeast**). It has many uses, for example as a cleaning fluid, and as liquid fuel.

Alcohol is also a drug and is found in alcoholic drinks, such as beer and wine, and spirits such as vodka.

albino noun and adjective

An albino is an animal or person with no colouring pigment in the skin and hair. (Pigment is the chemical that gives animals and humans colour.) An albino person has pale skin and white or light yellow hair. An albino's eyes are colourless, but they appear pink

All these drinks contain alcohol.

algae plural noun

(singular **alga**)

Algae are plants that grow mostly in water, and have no real stems or leaves. Seaweed is a kind of algae; so are the microscopic plants that make pond and river water green or murky.

alimentary canal noun

The alimentary canal is the long tube inside the bodies of animals, in which food is **digested**. The canal goes from the mouth to the **anus**.

See also: **digestive system**.

alive adjective

Being alive means being able to perform **life processes** such as feeding, breathing and growing.

See also: **dead**.

alkali noun

An alkali is a material, such as soda or ammonia that dissolves in water to make a bitter, soapy mixture. Alkalis turn red litmus paper blue. When an alkali is added to an acid, it cancels out (or neutralizes) the effect of the acid; the alkali in toothpaste neutralizes the acid that causes the teeth to decay.

See also: **acid**.

alkaline adjective This is used to describe materials, such as soil, which have a lot of alkali in them.

allergy noun

Having an allergy means being sensitive to something in the environment, such as **pollen**, or to certain foods, such as nuts. Allergies may cause reactions like sneezing, skin rashes, or **asthma**.

allergic adjective A person who has an allergy is described as being allergic to something. The effect an allergy has on someone is called an allergic reaction.

Hay fever is an allergy caused by pollen in summertime.

alloy noun

An alloy is a mixture of two metals. Bronze, for example, is an alloy of copper and tin, which are pure metals.

aluminium noun

Aluminium is a very light, silvery-coloured **metal**. Because of its lightness it is used, for example, in the building of bicycle and aeroplane parts. As it is also flexible, and a good **conductor** of electricity (electricity passes through it easily) it is used for overhead power lines.

ammonite noun

The picture shows the **fossil** (remains) of an ammonite – a small sea creature that lived in the seas and oceans around 120 million years ago.

4cm

amp (ampere) noun

Amp is short for **ampere**, which is the standard unit of electrical **current**. It is named after the French scientist, André-Marie Ampère.

amphibian noun

Amphibians are **cold-blooded** animals, such as frogs, toads and newts, which can live in water and on land. The young have **gills**, which enable them to breathe underwater, but when they become adult they develop air-breathing **lungs**.

Tadpole - has gills and lives in water.

Tadpole develops legs.

Frog - lives in water and on land, has lungs.

See also: **life cycle**.

amphibious adjective A creature that can live in water or on land, or a vehicle that can travel on water as well as land, is described as amphibious.

amplify verb

Amplify means to make something larger or stronger. For example, an **amplifier** on a CD player makes the electric signal stronger, so that the sound output is louder.

A

amplitude noun

See: **wave**.

anaesthetic noun

Anaesthetics are given to people and animals to stop them experiencing pain, for example during an operation. There are two kinds of anaesthetic: a local anaesthetic, which numbs part of the body but leaves the patient awake; and a general anaesthetic, which puts the patient to sleep.

analogue adjective

(**analog** in the USA)
Clocks, scales or other instruments that show information on a dial, or with a pointer, are described as analogue. This is different from a **digital** display, which uses only numbers.

digital
scales

analogue
scales

annual adjective

Annual means lasting for a year or happening once in a year.
An **annual plant** (or annual) is one that grows for one year or season only.

antibiotic noun

Antibiotics are materials produced by some **fungi** or **bacteria**, and are useful in treating illness. They can kill infections (caused by bacteria) but not **viruses**.

anticlockwise adverb

(in the USA, **counter-clockwise**)
When something turns in the opposite direction to the hands of a clock, it is moving anticlockwise.

See also: **clockwise**.

antiseptic noun

An antiseptic is a material that can destroy **bacteria** and stop wounds from becoming **septic** or infected.

antiseptic adjective This means clean and free of germs.

anus noun

The anus is the opening at the end of the **digestive system**, through which solid waste matter leaves the body.

aquatic adjective

Animals and plants that live or grow in water are described as aquatic. A dolphin is an aquatic **mammal**.

A dolphin is an aquatic mammal.

archaeology noun

Archaeology is the scientific study of ancient peoples from the remains of their buildings and their belongings.

artery noun

Arteries are tubes that carry the blood from the heart to the lungs and then to all other parts of the body.

As the heart pumps blood through the arteries, a **pulse** can be felt where an artery is close to the skin, for example in the wrist or neck.

See also: **circulatory system**, **vein**.

asteroid noun

There are many small rocks or broken parts of planets, mostly orbiting the Sun between Mars and Jupiter. These are called asteroids.

asthma noun

Asthma is a disease that causes difficulty with breathing. It is often caused by an **allergy**, for example to animal hairs, and can be helped by using an **inhaler**.

astronomy noun

Astronomy is the study of planets, stars and **galaxies**. In earlier times astronomers made their observations with the naked eye, but today they can work from buildings called **observatories** and use powerful instruments, such as **telescopes**, **satellites** and **computers**.

atmosphere noun

All the gases (or **air**) surrounding the Earth make up the atmosphere. Scientists describe the atmosphere as layers of gases, which become gradually thinner the higher they are above the Earth. The lowest layer, which is called the troposphere, contains the air we breathe. The ionosphere merges into the exosphere at around 900 km. Beyond the atmosphere is space.

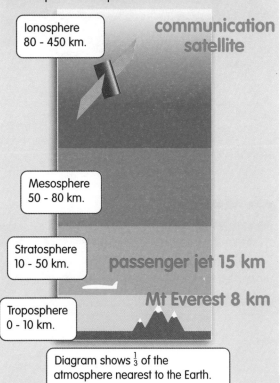

Ionosphere
80 - 450 km.

communication satellite

Mesosphere
50 - 80 km.

Stratosphere
10 - 50 km.

passenger jet 15 km

Mt Everest 8 km

Troposphere
0 - 10 km.

Diagram shows $\frac{1}{3}$ of the atmosphere nearest to the Earth.

A

atom noun

All materials are made up of billions of tiny **particles** called atoms. Each atom has a central part called the nucleus with a number of even tinier electrons surrounding it.

See also: **molecule**.

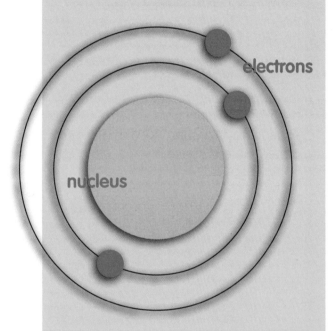

electrons

nucleus

attraction noun

Attraction is the name for the force that pulls things together. Magnets **attract** metal objects. The opposite of attract is **repel**.

axis noun

When an object spins like a top, the line it spins around is called an axis. Planet Earth spins on its axis once every 24 hours. As it spins, the Sun appears to rise and set, making day and night. The axis passes roughly through the North Pole and the South Pole.

The Earth's axis also tilts slightly. This causes the changing **seasons**.

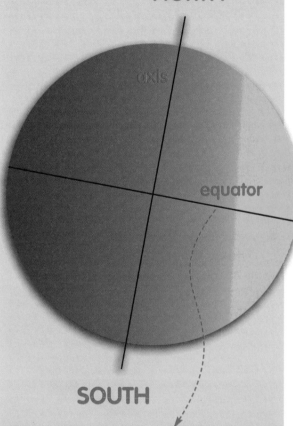

NORTH

axis

equator

SOUTH

The **equator** is an imaginary line round the Earth at an equal distance from the North and the South Poles.

bacteria   plural noun

(singular: bacterium)
Bacteria are tiny living things that are too small to see without a microscope, so we describe them as micro-organisms, or microbes. They live and reproduce inside human and animal bodies, in the environment (for example in soil or water) or in waste material. Some bacteria are useful, for example in making cheese or digesting food; others (which we call germs) are harmful and cause illness.

See also: microbe.

Magnified bacteria of the sort found in live yoghurt.

ball and socket joint   noun

This is part of an animal skeleton, where the rounded end of one bone fits into a hollow in another bone. It allows movement in all directions. In humans the shoulder and hip are ball and socket joints.

See also: hinge joint.

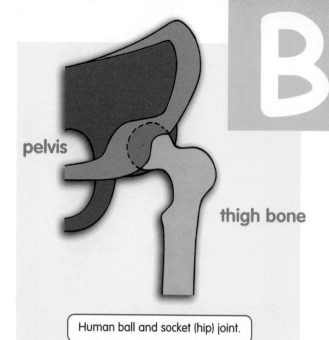

pelvis

thigh bone

Human ball and socket (hip) joint.

barometer   noun

A barometer is an instrument that measures air pressure. Air pressure changes according to the weather: high pressure usually means calm, fine weather; low pressure can mean storms. A barometer is basically a metal box from which most of the air has been taken out and a partial vacuum created. The result is that when the air pressure rises it pushes on the sides of the box and makes a pointer on the top of the box move in one direction. (It moves in the opposite direction if the air pressure falls.)

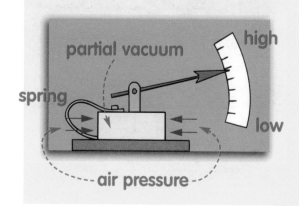

partial vacuum

high

spring

low

air pressure

11

B

basalt noun

Basalt is a hard, dark-coloured rock that is formed when volcanic lava cools. Sometimes, when it cools very quickly, by flowing into the sea, basalt forms into hexagonal columns, like those in Northern Ireland called the Giant's Causeway.

See also: igneous rock.

The Giant's Causeway is made up of irregular hexagons of basalt.

battery noun

A battery produces electricity from chemicals stored inside it. When a battery is connected by wires to a bulb, an electrical current flows through the wires and makes the bulb light up. Batteries can also be used to make buzzers sound and motors run.

The scientific name for a single battery is an electrical cell. A large battery, such as a car battery, may contain several cells.

Batteries (electrical cells).

beam noun

When we switch on a torch, light travels from the bulb in a beam. Sunlight shining through a slit or hole also travels in a beam.

A beam of light or other radiation is also called a **ray**.

belemnite noun

Belemnites are fossils of a sea creature that lived in the oceans millions of years ago. Belemnites are now **extinct**.

Fossil belemnite.

biennial adjective and noun

This word describes something that lasts for two years, or happens every two years.

Plants that grow leaves in the first year and produce flowers and fruit in the second year, and then die, are called **biennials**.

binocular vision noun

Animals that have two eyes which they can focus on an object have binocular vision. Humans have binocular vision.

binoculars plural noun

An instrument like a pair of telescopes, one for each eye, for **magnifying** distant objects.

biochemistry noun

This is a branch of science to do with the chemicals that living things are made of.

Bio– is a prefix meaning 'to do with life'.

biodegradable adjective

Something that is biodegradable is made from plants or animals and can rot away naturally through the action of **microbes**. An apple is biodegradable; so is a brown paper bag, and so are animals, but a plastic bag and a glass bottle are non-biodegradable.

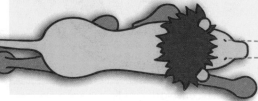

biology noun

Biology is the science and study of plants and animals and other living things.

biotechnology noun

Biotechnology is the way we use living things, especially micro-organisms, such as bacteria and fungi, to make useful products. For example, the manufacturing of cheese and yoghurt, wine, beer and bread are all forms of biotechnology. So is the producing of GM (genetically modified) food.

See also: genetic engineering.

Man adding rennet to milk to make cheese.

bird noun

Birds are animals with two legs, a pair of wings, and a body that is covered with feathers. Most birds can fly, using their wings.

Birds are members of the animal kingdom. They are vertebrates, which means they have a backbone (or spine). Female birds lay eggs, from which young birds hatch.

black hole noun

Some stars are so massive that nothing can escape from the pull of gravity near them – not even their own light. As no light leaves them, they appear dark; astronomers therefore call them black holes.

blood noun

Blood is the red liquid that is pumped around a body by the heart. It travels through tubes called blood vessels, and carries oxygen from the lungs, and nutrients from food, to all parts of the body where they are needed. It also gathers up waste materials, so that they can be removed from the body.

The main parts of blood are plasma, which is the liquid, red cells which carry the nutrients, and white cells which fight germs.

Human blood: blood cells float in liquid plasma.

blood transfusion   noun

When a person loses a lot of blood, it needs to be replaced, and so the person is given a blood transfusion.

Blood is taken from a storage container and pumped into a person's veins. Many people (called blood donors) give some of their blood to be stored in a blood 'bank' until it is needed.

blood vessel   noun

Blood vessels are tubes inside the body that connect the heart to other parts of the body so that blood can circulate. Arteries are large blood vessels that carry blood away from the heart; veins are large blood vessels that carry blood towards the heart.

Capillaries are tiny blood vessels that branch off from the main network of vessels to carry blood to cells in the body.

boil   verb

When a liquid reaches a certain temperature, bubbles of vapour (gas) form, then rise to the surface and escape. This is called boiling.

Boiling point noun The temperature at which a liquid starts to boil and becomes a gas is called its boiling point. The boiling point of water is 100 °C (degrees Celsius). Some liquids have lower boiling points than this; some higher. Once a liquid has reached boiling point, its temperature will not rise any higher, as all the heat energy is used up in turning the liquid into vapour.

See also: evaporate.

botany   noun

Botany is the study of plants, and is a branch of biology.

See also: zoology.

bronchial   adjective

The tubes which carry air down into the lungs are called the bronchial tubes. They branch out into smaller tubes called bronchioles.

bronchitis   noun

If the bronchial tubes, which lead down into the lungs, become inflamed (infected and sore), this causes coughing and breathing difficulties. This condition is called bronchitis.

bud   noun

Buds are the first signs of a leaf or flower on a plant.

bud verb When a plant buds, this means it is starting to show buds.

bulb noun

Some plants, for example tulips and onions, have a stem that swells up into a rounded shape called a bulb. Inside the bulb are the shoots that will grow into a new plant, and a store of nutrients (food).

Cross-section of a bulb.

Bunsen burner noun

This is a small burner used in laboratories to heat substances quickly. It produces a hot flame from a mixture of gas and air. The gas is fed in through a pipe and the air is let in through holes in the base. It was named after Robert Bunsen, who invented it.

----- air inlet

gas supply

Bunsen burner.

buoyant adjective

Something that is buoyant floats in a liquid, or rises in the air. Boats are buoyant in water; a helium balloon is buoyant in the air.

An object is buoyant if it weighs less than the same volume of the liquid or gas it is in. The weight of the liquid or gas forces the lighter object upwards.

buoyancy noun This is the property of being buoyant, or of being able to float.

burn verb

Burning is caused by heat. When materials burn, they change. For example, when wood burns, it changes into charcoal.

See also: combustion (which is a more scientific word for burning).

calcium noun

Pure calcium is a silvery-coloured, fairly hard metal. It is found in the bones, claws and teeth of animals, and in shells. Humans need to have some calcium in their diet to stay healthy. Eggs and milk are two of the foods that contain calcium.

Calcium occurs in limestone, chalk and marble. It can be mixed with other materials to make many useful products, including plaster and cement.

callipers plural noun

An instrument with two curved arms hinged at one end, used for measuring the width of tubes or round objects, or gaps between surfaces.

calorie noun

A calorie is a unit of heat energy. It is used especially to measure the amount of energy provided by food.

camera noun

A camera is an instrument for taking photographs. It is a light-proof box, which can hold special light-sensitive paper, or 'film'. A small hole, or a lens, fitted with a 'shutter', is opened for a short time, so that light from an object outside the camera can be focused on to the film. This creates a photograph.

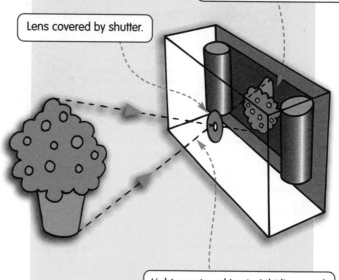

Light-sensitive film on a roll.

Lens covered by shutter.

Light rays travel in straight lines and cross over one another at the point at which they enter the camera. The whole image appears upside-down on the film.

How a camera works.

A movie camera takes a series of photographs very quickly, one after another, so that the images appear to move.

camouflage   noun

Some animals have colouring that makes them difficult to see against their usual background. This is called camouflage.

This gecko is camouflaged against a leaf.

cancer   noun

Cancer is a disease that is caused by abnormal cells (tiny parts) in the body dividing and spreading to form growths called tumours.

Cancer can affect many parts of the body, including the lungs, the stomach, bones and even skin. Exposure to strong sunlight can cause skin cancer. Smoking is known to be a cause of lung cancer.

canine   adjective

This word is used to describe things that are to do with dogs. Human canine teeth, for example, are sharp, pointed teeth that are good for gripping and tearing food, and are similar to those that dogs have.

carbohydrate   noun

A carbohydrate is an energy-giving substance made by green plants. It is made up of carbon, hydrogen, and oxygen. Foods that contain carbohydrate include pasta, bread, rice and potatoes.

carbon   noun

Carbon is a material that comes in many forms, including diamond, graphite (pencil 'lead'), and charcoal (a black or dark grey substance used as a fuel in barbecues).

All known living things contain carbon and other materials, such as oxygen and hydrogen. Plants, for example, consist of carbon, oxygen and hydrogen. Fossil fuels, such as coal and oil, also contain carbon.

carbon cycle   noun

Carbon in atmosphere.

Plants use carbon dioxide from the atmosphere to photosynthesise.

Burning of fossil fuels.

Organisms produce carbon dioxide, through respiration.

Photosynthesis.

Microscopic creatures in the soil use carbon dioxide.

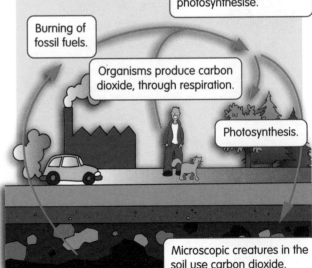

carbon dioxide noun

Carbon dioxide is a gas. We cannot see it or smell it, but it is present in the air around us.

Carbon dioxide is produced when carbon and oxygen join together. This happens when fuel is burned. For example, when a candle is lit, carbon in the wax joins with oxygen in the air, making carbon dioxide. Carbon dioxide bubbles are also produced when yeast is mixed with bread dough or fruit juice.

Humans and other animals produce carbon dioxide from the carbon they get from food and the oxygen they breathe in. This carbon dioxide is then breathed out into the air. (See: respiration.) Green plants do the opposite: they absorb carbon dioxide from the air and split it into carbon and oxygen. They store the carbon in their leaves as food and release the oxygen into the air. (See: photosynthesis.)

Carbon dioxide is heavier than other gases in the air; therefore it settles close to the ground. It does not burn like many gases do, and is therefore useful for putting out fires. Its full name is often shortened to CO_2, because each molecule is made of one carbon atom and two oxygen atoms.

carcinogenic adjective

Carcinogenic materials are those that cause or increase the risk of developing cancer.

carcinogen noun A carcinogen is a cancer-causing substance.

carnivore noun

A carnivore is an animal that eats meat.

See also: herbivore, omnivore.

cell noun

A cell is the smallest organism (living thing) or smallest part of an organism. Some micro-organisms, such as bacteria, are single-celled. Animals and plants are made of millions of cells of different kinds: for example, blood cells, skin cells, and brain cells.

A single battery is also called a cell. To be accurate, battery means two or more cells joined together.

Celsius scale noun

Anders Celsius was the Swedish scientist who invented a standard scale for measuring temperature. He took the freezing point of water as zero degrees and the boiling point of water as 100 degrees. Temperatures below the freezing point of water are given as negative numbers on the scale. The symbol for a degree is °. Twenty degrees Celsius is written 20 °C.

chalk noun

Chalk is a soft, white rock, containing calcium. Chalk crumbles easily, but does not dissolve in water.

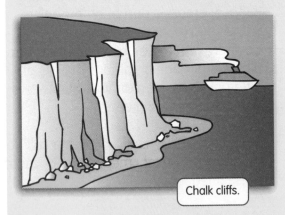

Chalk cliffs.

characteristic noun

This word has a similar meaning to 'property'. Describing characteristics tells us what something is like. For example, being soft and crumbly are characteristics of chalk.

chemical change noun

A chemical change takes place when materials react with each other to make new materials.

See also: irreversible change, reaction.

chemistry noun

Chemistry is the study of materials and their properties (what they are like). It is also about the reactions between materials (the way they affect each other and produce new substances).

chlorophyll noun

A green pigment (colouring) found in plants.

See also: photosynthesis.

circuit noun

Anything that goes round in a complete loop is called a circuit. A race track, for example, is often a circuit.

An electrical circuit is formed when wires connect a power source, such as a battery, to a component such as a bulb or motor, and back to the power source. This allows a current to flow, which lights the bulb or powers the motor.

A circuit diagram is a diagram showing the components and the wires connecting them.

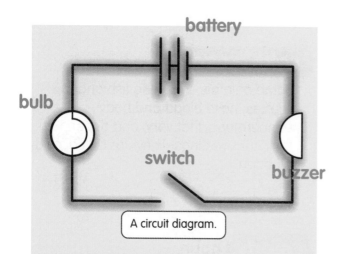

battery

bulb

switch

buzzer

A circuit diagram.

circuit symbol noun

A circuit symbol is a small diagram of a
component in an electrical **circuit**, for
example a bulb or battery, used in
drawing circuit diagrams.

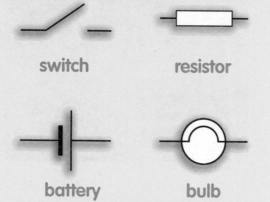

switch

resistor

battery

bulb

circulatory system noun

This is the name given to the system of
tubes that carry the **blood** around the
body. At the centre of the system is the
heart, which pumps the blood through
arteries to the **lungs** and to the
muscles and other organs in the body,
where oxygen and nutrients are needed.
The arteries branch into thinner and
thinner tubes, so that the blood can
reach all parts. The smallest of these are
called capillaries.

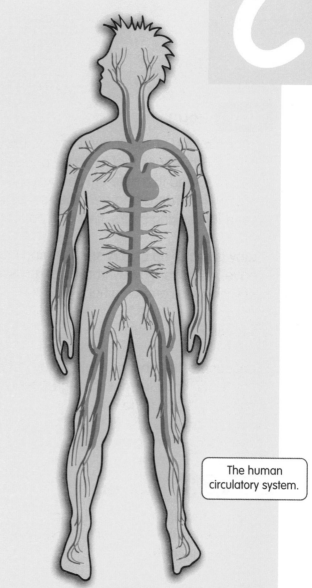

The human
circulatory system.

See also: vein.

classify verb

To sort a collection of things into groups
that share similar characteristics is to
classify them.

A part of science is the classification of all
living things into groups or classes.

See also: kingdom.

clay noun

Clay is a kind of soil. When it is wet, it is soft, which means that it can be pressed and moulded into different shapes. When it is dry it hardens and becomes solid. It is used for making bricks, tiles and pottery.

Clay is made up of very small grains that have been worn away from large masses of rock by ice and weather.

See also: sediment.

Because of its very fine grains, clay does not allow water to soak through easily, as some soils and sand do.

See also: permeable.

clockwise adverb

When something turns in the same direction as the hands of a clock, it is moving clockwise.

See also: anticlockwise.

coal noun

Coal is a hard, black material that is burned as fuel, to provide warmth and to produce energy.

See also: fossil fuel.

cold-blooded adjective

Some animals, including fish and reptiles, have blood and body temperatures that vary, and depend on their surroundings. They are called 'cold-blooded'.

See also: warm-blooded.

colony noun

A colony is a group of animals or plants of the same kind that live and grow together. Corals, sponges, bees, ants, and termites all live in colonies.

Honey bees on a honeycomb.

combustion noun

Combustion is the scientific word for burning. When a fuel burns (or combusts) it reacts with oxygen in the air. Usually it takes heat to start combustion, but once this has begun, more heat is produced, which keeps combustion going until the fuel or the oxygen is used up.

Combustion is usually accompanied by flames, which are hot, burning gases. A material that is capable of being lit and burning is combustible.

comet noun

Comets are clusters of gas and debris that orbit the Sun. However, their orbits are elliptical (oval-shaped) and off-centre, so that after passing close to the Sun, the comets travel far out into space before returning many years or even centuries later. Comets have a 'head' which is thought to be solid. When they are near the Sun they grow a 'tail' of luminous **vapour**, which streams out away from the Sun.

The most famous comet is Halley's Comet, which visits the solar system every 76 years, and was last seen in 1986.

Halley's comet.

compass noun

A compass is an instrument with a magnetized needle, balanced so that it swings to face roughly north. People on boats, ships, and aircraft, as well as hill-walkers and explorers use compasses to help them find their way.

If they know where north is, then they can work out where south, east and west are and decide in which direction they need to travel.

See also: **magnet**.

component noun

A single part of a system is called a component. In an electrical circuit, for example, bulbs, buzzers, motors, etc. are the components.

compost noun

When living **matter**, such as leaves and vegetables, dies and **decays**, it becomes compost.

See also: **biodegradable**.

compound

adjective and noun

Compound means made of more than one part. Water is a compound because it is made of two **elements**: oxygen and hydrogen.

compress verb

To compress something is to squash it, so that it takes up less space. For example, when air is pumped into a bicycle tyre it is under pressure, and is **compressed**.

computer noun

A computer is an electronic machine that can do calculations (sums) and process (use) **data** (information) at high speed.

C

concave adjective

A shape that is concave is curved inwards, like the inside of a dish. A lens or a mirror is described as concave if its surface is this shape.

See also: **convex** and **lens**.

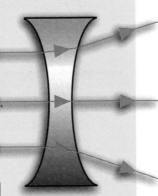

light ray

Light rays spread (diverge) as they pass through a concave lens.

conclusion noun

A conclusion is a decision we come to after thinking carefully and looking at facts or evidence. For example, after touching several different metal objects with a magnet, we are likely to reach the conclusion that some metals are attracted by magnets, while others are not.

The verb 'draw' is often used with 'conclusion'. For example, 'Lucy drew the conclusion that not all metals are magnetic.'

conclude verb This means to reach or draw a conclusion.

condense verb

When **vapour** cools and becomes liquid, it condenses. Water vapour (steam) condenses into droplets of water when it touches a cool surface, such as a bathroom mirror.

condensation noun This is the liquid that forms when a vapour condenses.

See also: **evaporation**.

Steam from a shower creates condensation on a mirror.

conductor noun

Heat, sound, and electricity travel easily through some materials; we call these materials conductors. For example, copper is a good conductor of electricity and heat. A **lightning conductor** is a metal rod placed on tall buildings and connected to the earth. If it is struck by lightning, it conducts the electricity safely down into the ground.

conduct verb Some materials conduct heat, electricity, or sound better than others. For example, a metal spoon conducts heat well, so the handle starts to feel hot when we stir a cup of tea. Polystyrene foam is a very poor conductor of heat; fast-food outlets often serve hot drinks in polystyrene cups because the heat inside a polystyrene cup does not travel to the outside of the cup, where it could burn our fingers.

See also:
insulator.

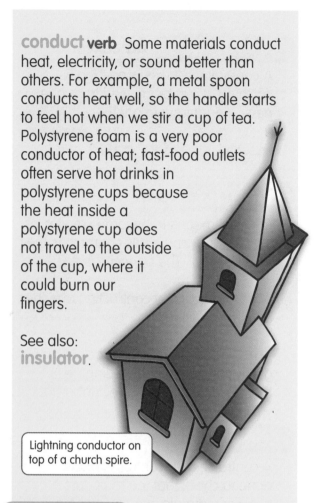

Lightning conductor on top of a church spire.

coniferous adjective

A coniferous tree (or conifer) is one that grows cones and has thin spiky leaves. Pine and fir trees are conifers. Most, but not all coniferous trees, are **evergreen**: they keep their leaves/needles in winter.

connection noun

An electrical connection is a place where wires are joined to a **component**, such as a battery or bulb holder.

connect verb This means to make a connection.

conservation noun

Conservation means keeping something the same, or stopping it from being destroyed. The protection of the **environment** (for example the countryside, forests, rivers) and of plant and animal species that are in danger of being lost, is called conservation.

conserve verb This means to keep or protect.

conservationist noun
A conservationist is someone who believes strongly in conserving the environment.

constellation noun

A constellation is a group of stars, which form an imaginary shape in the night sky. The word 'stellar' (adjective) means 'to do with stars'. (Both 'stellar' and 'constellation' come from 'stella', which is the Latin word for star.)

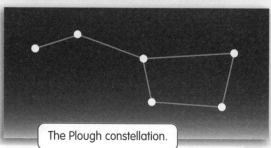

The Plough constellation.

consumer noun

In a food chain a consumer is an animal that gets its food from a plant or other animal.

If a caterpillar eats a leaf, it is called the first consumer. If a bird eats the caterpillar, it is called the second consumer, and so on. The plant is called the producer.

See also: predator.

consume verb This means to eat or use up.

contact noun

Part of an electric circuit where one conductor touches another is called a contact. When the conductors touch, they 'make contact' and allow the electric current to flow. If the contact is 'broken', for example inside a switch, the current stops flowing.

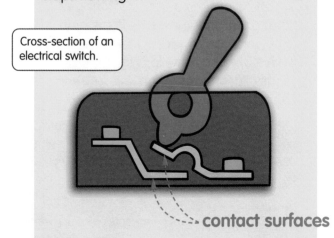

Cross-section of an electrical switch.

contact surfaces

contagious adjective

A contagious illness is one that is catching; it can be passed from one person or animal to another.

See also: infection, virus.

contract verb

Contract means to become smaller, or shrink. Many materials contract as they become cool. The opposite is expand.

Muscles work by contracting and then relaxing.

contraction noun Contraction means getting smaller, or squeezing or tightening as in a muscle contraction.

control adjective and noun

A control test (or control) is one that is done to check that the main test is a fair test. For example, we could show that direct sunlight speeds up evaporation (drying) by placing a saucer of water in the sun; but we would have to place another with the same amount of water in the shade to make a comparison with the first saucer. The saucer in the shade would be the control saucer.

See also: fair test.

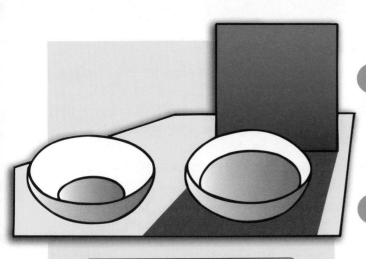

This control test shows that water does not dry up as quickly out of the sun.

convex adjective

A shape that is convex is curved outwards, or bulges. A lens or a mirror is called convex if its surface is this shape.

See also: concave, lens.

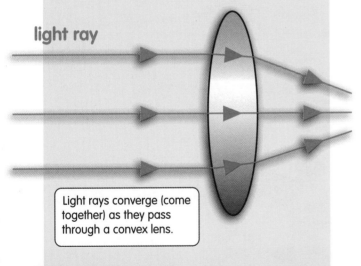

light ray

Light rays converge (come together) as they pass through a convex lens.

copper noun

Copper is a fairly soft, reddish-brown metal. It is an excellent conductor of electricity and heat, and is used to make electric wiring.

core noun

The solid material at the centre of the Earth is called the core.

See also: Earth.

crust noun

When molten rock or other material cools, it hardens, becomes a solid and forms a crust.

See also: Earth.

crystal noun

Many materials form into crystals, which are straight-edged and 3-dimensional shapes with flat faces that sparkle when they reflect light. Diamonds are crystals; so are snowflakes.

crystallize verb When something crystallizes, it forms into crystals.

crystalline adjective A material that is crystalline forms into crystals or is composed of crystals. Salt and quartz are crystalline.

crystallization noun This is the process of forming crystals.

Crystals of amethyst.

current noun

When something flows, it is called a current. There are currents of water in rivers, and tidal currents in the sea.

The flow of electricity through a wire is also called current, and is measured in amperes.

cycle noun

A cycle is a series of happenings that repeats itself over and over again. For example, the seasons (spring, summer, autumn, winter) come around in a cycle.

See also: carbon cycle, life cycle, menstrual cycle, water cycle.

cyclic adjective Events, like the seasons, that happen in a cycle are described as cyclic or cyclical.

summer

spring

The cycle of the seasons.

autumn

winter

dairy product noun

Dairy products are made from cows', sheep's or goats' milk. Butter, cheese, and yoghurt are all examples of dairy products.

dairy noun A dairy is a place where dairy products are produced or sold.

Dairy products.

data plural noun

Data is information, especially information that is used for making decisions or solving problems. The information is often in the form of numbers or graphs and diagrams.

database noun A database is a store of data, usually in a computer, in which we can search for information.

See also: graph.

dead adjective

A plant or animal is dead when it can no longer carry out life processes, such as feeding and breathing. Dead things should not be confused with things that have never been alive.

decay verb and noun

When something decays, it rots. Dead plants decay and become compost. Microbes, such as bacteria, cause decay. Heat and moisture also speed up decay.

decibel noun

(abbreviation dB)
A decibel is a unit used to measure the volume (loudness) of sounds.

Decibels are named after Alexander Graham Bell, the inventor of the telephone.

Sound over 100 decibels can be painful and damaging to the ear.

D

deciduous — adjective

Deciduous trees shed their leaves in autumn, and grow new leaves in spring.

decompose — verb

Decompose means to rot or **decay**.

decomposer noun A decomposer is a living thing, such as a **fungus** or a **microbe** that causes dead animals and plants to rot.

defecation — noun

This is the expelling of solid waste (called **faeces**) from the body at the end of the digestion process.

degree — noun

A degree is a unit of measurement. A circle, for example, is divided into 360 degrees. Temperature is also measured in degrees. The symbol for a degree is °.

See also: **Celsius scale**.

dehydrate — verb

Dehydrate means to lose water. Plants that are not watered become dehydrated, as do humans and animals that have not had enough to drink.

dehydration noun If someone is suffering from dehydration it means they have lost a lot of water and have not replaced it. Hot sun, sweating, diarrhoea, and being sick can all cause dehydration. So can some **drugs**. If not treated, dehydration can cause death.

dense — adjective

Dense means thick, heavy, solid. Wood is more dense than sponge, but less dense than iron or lead. Liquids and solids are denser than gases. Some materials can be made more dense through being compressed (squashed). Large volumes of gas, for example, can be **compressed** into a small cylinder. When the gas escapes it thins out and becomes less dense.

Gases can be made less dense by being heated, because they expand and take up more space. Hot air is therefore lighter than the same volume of cold air, which is why a hot air balloon rises when the air inside it is heated, and comes down again when it cools.

density noun Density means how much **mass** something has (and therefore how heavy it is) for its size.

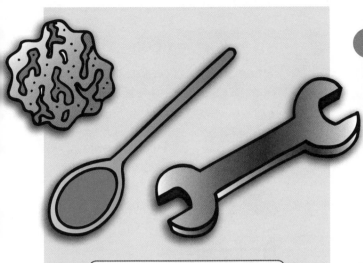

A sponge, wooden spoon and steel spanner all have different densities.

dentine noun

Dentine is a hard, dense bony material out of which the inside part of a tooth is made.

See also: teeth.

diet noun

The diet of a person or animal means everything that it eats. For example, grass is the diet of cows; fish is the diet of penguins.

The word is also used to mean the eating plan that someone follows when they are trying to lose weight or live more healthily.

digest verb

After food is eaten by humans and other animals, it is digested. This means that the useful materials are taken out of the food to be used for nourishment (to keep someone alive and well), while the rest is expelled as waste.

See also: digestive system.

digestion noun This is the process of digesting food.

digestive system noun

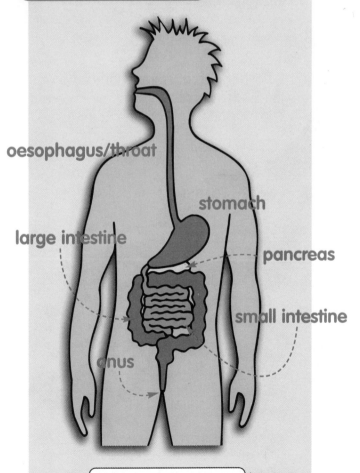

The human digestive system.

D

digital *adjective*

Digital means to do with numbers. For example, on a digital clock the time is shown by numbers that keep changing, rather than by hands that move round on the dial of an analogue clock.

Information or data that is stored in numbers, for example in a computer or on a CD, is called digital.

See also: **analogue**.

dinosaur *noun*

Dinosaurs were reptiles that lived on the Earth from around 250 million years ago up until around 65 million years ago. Their name, which comes from Greek, means 'terrible lizard'.

This dinosaur is called Tyrannosaurus rex. It grew to 12m in length and 6m in height.

disinfectant *noun*

A disinfectant is a chemical that kills **germs** (**bacteria** and **viruses**). It is used to clean surfaces to prevent the spread of **infection**. It is also put on wounds to fight infection.

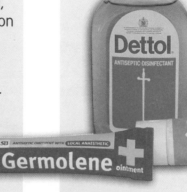

dispersal *noun*

Dispersal means scattering. It is used to describe the spreading of seeds by wind and by birds. Some plants have seed pods that explode and scatter the seeds.

dissolve *verb*

When a substance dissolves in a liquid, it mixes with it and becomes part of the liquid. For example, sugar and salt both dissolve in water.

When a **solid** has been dissolved, it cannot be separated again by **sieving**. However, liquids and dissolved solids can be separated by **boiling** or **evaporating** the liquid away to leave the solid behind.

32

distillation noun

Distillation occurs when a liquid is **evaporated** by **boiling** and then **condensed** back into a liquid by cooling. The result is a pure liquid, because it has been separated from impurities by the process of distillation. Distilled water, for example, has no salt or other minerals in it, even if it has been made from salt water.

diurnal adjective

Diurnal is used to describe things that happen once a day, or that happen during daytime rather than at night. Animals that are active in daylight hours are diurnal, as are plants with flowers that open in the daytime and close at night.

See also: **nocturnal**.

diversity noun

Diversity means difference. In science it is used to describe the huge variety of living things.

The diversity of life.

DNA abbreviation

These letters stand for deoxyribonucleic acid. This substance makes up our **genes** and passes on genetic information when living things reproduce (produce young).

See also: **generation**.

drought noun

Droughts occur when there is not enough rain. Rivers and streams dry up and crops die, often resulting in humans and animals dying from lack of food and water.

Dead cow during a drought in Kenya.

drug noun

A drug is any substance, other than food or water, that is put into the body and changes a person's physical or mental state in some way.

These changes can be helpful or harmful. For example, drugs taken regularly for asthma can be helpful, but drinking too much alcohol can be harmful.

E

ear noun

The ear is the **organ** in humans and many other animals that senses sound. Inside the ear is a small piece of tightly-stretched skin, called the ear-drum. Sound waves in the air make this skin vibrate (move quickly to and fro). **Nerves** connected to the inner ear carry the vibrations to the brain, which recognizes them as sound.

The ear also contains three small, semi-circular canals (tubes) which control balance.

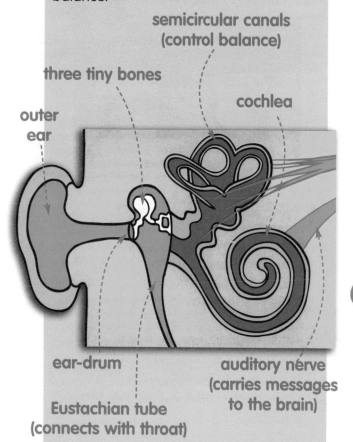

semicircular canals
(control balance)

three tiny bones

cochlea

outer
ear

ear-drum

auditory nerve
(carries messages
to the brain)

Eustachian tube
(connects with throat)

Earth noun

The Earth is the planet that we live on. It is roughly spherical (ball-shaped) but flattened slightly at the north and south poles, like an orange.

The Earth spins like a top, once every 24 hours (a day), from west to east, around an **axis** running roughly from the North to the South Pole. It also travels in an **orbit** around the Sun once every $365\frac{1}{4}$ days (a year).

The Earth is made mostly of rock. On the surface this is solid, and is called the Earth's **crust**. Underneath where it is much hotter, it is **molten** (made into liquid by great heat). Right at the centre of the Earth there is a core that is thought to be solid.

earthquake noun

Earthquakes occur where there are cracks or faults in the Earth's crust. **Volcanic** pressure underneath can cause movement. This makes the ground above shudder, or quake. Earthquakes can cause serious damage and great loss of life.

The strength of an earthquake is measured on a scale called the Richter Scale from 1–10; the higher the number, the more severe the earthquake.

echo noun

When sound waves hit a surface they are reflected, and can return a few seconds later to where the sound came from. Because of the time this takes, the reflected sound is heard as an echo.

echo sounder noun

This is an instrument that uses echoes to measure the depth of water. This system is also called sonar.

eclipse noun and verb

An eclipse happens when a large object in space blocks the light from another, causing a shadow. For example, when the Moon comes between the Earth and the Sun, there is an eclipse of the Sun (a **solar** eclipse). When the Earth comes between the Sun and the Moon, it casts a shadow on the Moon (a **lunar** eclipse).

When the whole of the Sun is eclipsed it is called a 'total eclipse'. When part of it is hidden, it is called a 'partial eclipse'.

A total solar eclipse.

ecology noun

Ecology is the study of the **environment** and the effects that humans have on it.

ecosystem noun

An ecosystem is a single part of the **environment**, together with the living things that belong to it and depend on it. For example, an island and all its inhabitants could form a complete ecosystem, as could an oak tree, a hedge, a pond or an ocean.

E

edible adjective

Something that is edible is something that can be eaten. The opposite is 'inedible'.

egg noun

An egg begins life as a single cell (tiny piece of matter) that is produced by a female. Once fertilized by a male cell, the egg is able to develop into a new plant or animal.

In most mammals, the egg is fertilized and develops inside the female's body. Mammals then give birth to live young.

Birds, reptiles and insects lay eggs that have hard shells and contain a food source (yolk) for the developing young.

The eggs of fish and amphibians are laid in water and do not have hard shells.

electricity noun

Electricity is a source of power. It is used to produce light, heat, sound, and motion. Electricity can be generated by burning fuel in power stations, or from natural forces such as wind and water, or from the heat of the Sun. It can also be obtained from batteries.

There is electricity in all matter in the form of electric charge (the amount of electricity contained in something). If this charge moves, for example along a wire, it is called a current. When wires are connected to a battery to form a complete circuit, an electric current is produced and moves along the wire. Electricity that is supplied to homes and factories is called 'mains' electricity. It is very powerful; touching mains wiring can cause serious injury or death.

electric adjective (or electrical)

These words describe things that have electricity in them or are powered by electricity. For example, electric charge, electric motor.

electromagnet noun

If a wire carrying an electric current is wound around a metal bar, the bar becomes a magnet. It is only a temporary magnet because it loses its magnetism if the current is switched off.

See also: magnet.

Powerful electromagnets can be used to lift heavy metal objects. They also provide the force that drives electric motors.

electromagnetic spectrum noun

The electromagnetic spectrum is made up of different electromagnetic waves (radiation), including visible light. Some waves have shorter wavelengths than light:
- gamma rays
- X-rays
- ultraviolet rays.

Some have longer wavelengths:
- infra-red rays
- radio waves.

All the wavelengths, from the longest to the shortest, form the **spectrum** (range) of electromagnetic radiation.

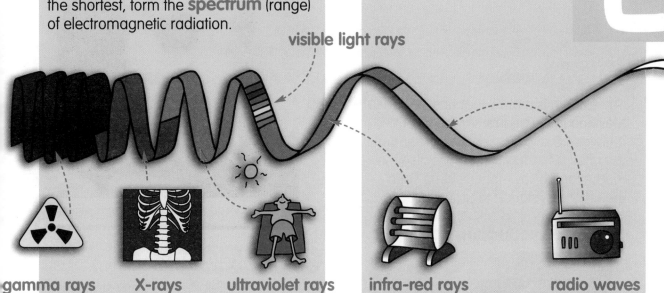

visible light rays

gamma rays   X-rays   ultraviolet rays   infra-red rays   radio waves

electron   noun

See **atom**.

electron microscope   noun

An electron microscope is one that uses **electrons** (tiny particles within an atom) instead of visible light to magnify objects. It can create images of particles that are too small to be detected by an **optical** microscope (a microscope with lenses, of the type that is used in schools).

electronic   adjective

This word describes any device or machine that is run and controlled by electricity, for example computers, or mobile phones.

electronics noun This is the study of anything electronic.

element   noun

All material is made of **atoms**. If the atoms are all of one kind, the material is called an element. There are over 100 known elements, including carbon, gold, hydrogen, iron, lead, oxygen and sodium.

Materials that contain two or more different elements are called **compounds**.

E

embryo noun

An embryo is a baby that has started to develop in the mother's **womb** and is between 0 and 8 weeks old. (After that it is called a **foetus**.) Embryo is also the name for the tiny plant inside a seed before it has started to grow.

See also: **reproduction**.

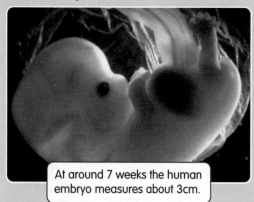

At around 7 weeks the human embryo measures about 3cm.

enamel noun

It is a hard, shiny material, which is often used to cover other materials, such as metal, to protect their surface. It also occurs naturally, for example, in the hard outer covering of our **teeth**, and is the hardest substance in the body.

endangered species noun

Animals or plants that are rare and at risk of becoming **extinct** (dying out) are called endangered species. Many living things are endangered because humans have destroyed or changed their **habitat** (the place where they live).

The giant panda is an endangered species.

endoskeleton noun

An endoskeleton is the bony structure that supports an animal's body from inside, and is covered by the muscles and skin. Mice, birds, fish, and humans are some of the animals with endoskeletons.

See also: **exoskeleton**, **skeleton**.

energy noun

Energy is what is needed to do any kind of work or to make things happen.

There are several different forms of energy (for example light, heat, sound, movement, electrical and chemical energy). One kind can become another. The energy in moving water can be used to turn a water wheel, which makes machinery work, or it can be used to turn a **turbine**, and so the energy is changed into electricity. The electrical energy can then be changed into heat energy, used to run motors, or to produce light or sound.

The energy in flowing water causes the water wheel to turn and this causes machinery to work.

Food provides us with energy to help us stay alive.

There is chemical energy in the food that we eat; we can use this to move or stay warm.

environment noun

The area around something is called its environment. Environments vary enormously: forest, mountain, and desert environments are all very different. Animals and plants have to **adapt** to suit their particular environment.

This bird has long legs to suit its swampy environment.

epidemic noun

A disease that spreads amongst a species and affects a large number of people or animals is called an epidemic. Foot-and-mouth disease caused a serious epidemic among farm animals in 2001.

equator noun

The equator is an imaginary horizontal line around the world midway between the North Pole and the South Pole.

See also: **axis**.

N

equator

S

equinox noun

The equinoxes are the two times in the year when day and night are the same length all over the world. The spring (or vernal) equinox is around 20 March; the autumn equinox takes place around 22 September.

E

erosion noun

Erosion is the gradual wearing away of rock or soil by water, wind or ice.

erode verb The crashing of waves against cliffs will gradually cause the cliffs to erode.

Erosion occurs at cliffs along the coast.

evaporate verb

A liquid evaporates when it changes into a gas or vapour. When a puddle dries up it is because water has evaporated into the air. Water also evaporates when it is boiled and turns into steam.

evaporation noun Evaporation is the process of liquid changing to vapour.

evergreen adjective

An evergreen tree is one that keeps its green leaves all year round.

See also: **coniferous, deciduous**.

evidence noun

Scientific evidence is information that scientists use to reach conclusions. **Fossil** remains, for example, are the evidence we have that dinosaurs once roamed the Earth.

evolution noun

Evolution is the slow development of different species over millions of years. The first simple forms of life have **evolved** into the countless different animals and plants that we see today.

excrete verb

Excreting is removing waste. It is one of the life processes common to all living things. Humans and other animals excrete waste in urine, in faeces, in perspiration (sweat) and in breath.

exercise noun and verb

Exercise uses up energy. It strengthens **muscles** and keeps bodies healthy.

exhale verb

To exhale means to breathe out by pushing air out of the lungs. It is the opposite of **inhale**.

exoskeleton noun

Some animals, for example crabs, lobsters and beetles, have a hard outer layer to protect and support them. This makes them different from animals with an **endoskeleton**.

A lobster.

expand verb

Expand means grow larger. Most materials expand as they are heated. The lungs expand as we inhale (or breathe in).

experiment noun and verb

Scientists carry out experiments to test their ideas. Scientific experiments can also lead to inventions. By experimenting with sound and electricity Alexander Graham Bell invented the telephone.

extinct adjective

A species becomes extinct (or goes into extinction) when the last one of its kind dies.

Dinosaurs became extinct millions of years ago.

Dodo - a flightless bird which became extinct in 1681.

eye noun

Eyes are **organs** that humans and many other animals have, which provide the sense of sight. The eyes focus light on to an area called the retina, which is sensitive to light. From here, messages are sent to the brain.

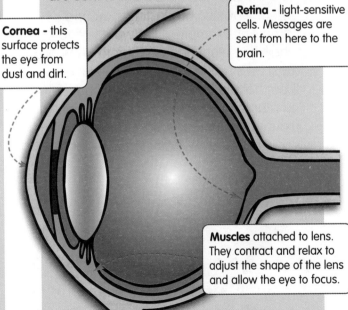

Cornea - this surface protects the eye from dust and dirt.

Retina - light-sensitive cells. Messages are sent from here to the brain.

Muscles attached to lens. They contract and relax to adjust the shape of the lens and allow the eye to focus.

Cross-section of a human eye.

Some animals, for example flies, have compound eyes; each eye is a cluster of many small eyes.

F

fabric   noun

Fabric is any cloth that has been woven or knitted.

faeces   plural noun

(pronounced fee-seez)
This is the name for the waste matter that is left in the large intestine at the end of digestion. It is expelled (pushed out) from the anus.

fair test   noun

To make a fair test (or a fair comparison) we have to make sure that everything except what we are testing stays the same. For example, if we want to find out whether a plant needs water to grow, we must take two identical plants, place them both in the same position, but only give water to one of them. Then if one plant grows and one does not, we will know for certain what has made the difference.

This is a fair test.

famine   noun

When the people of a country or region do not have enough to eat, this is called a famine. Famines can be caused by any of the following: crop diseases, a shortage of water, war, or overpopulation.

fats and oils   plural nouns

Fats and oils are an essential part of a healthy diet, and can be obtained from animals or from plant seeds. Fats and oils provide the body with energy. Fat provides a long-term energy store for the body. Too much fat, especially animal fat, can be harmful.

See also: diet, nutrient.

ferment   verb

When yeast is added to a liquid containing sugar, for example fruit juice, the mixture ferments: the sugar changes into carbon dioxide and alcohol, and the mixture froths and bubbles.

fermentation noun The process of fermenting.

See also: alcohol, yeast.

fern   noun

Ferns are a group of plants with feathery leaves. Ferns do not flower or produce seeds. They reproduce from spores (tiny cells) that develop on the underside of the leaves. The spores are microscopic (too small to be seen without a microscope) and can be carried by the wind to new areas of ground, where they can grow into new plants.

Ferns are often sold as house plants.

fertilization noun

Fertilization is the start of a new living thing: the first stage of **reproduction**. In animals it takes place when a male sperm joins with a female ovum (egg). In many land animals, such as mammals, this happens inside the body. In animals that reproduce in water, such as frogs, the eggs are fertilized outside the body. In plants it is the male **pollen** that fertilizes the female ovum.

fertilizer noun

Fertilizer is any chemical or **natural** substance which is added to soil to make plants stronger and healthier.

fertile adjective Soil in which plants grow well is fertile.

fibre noun

Fibres are thin, thread-like materials. If we look at wool or cotton wool under a magnifying lens, we can see the fibres matted together.

Foods, such as fruit and cereals that are high in fibre are an important part of a healthy **diet**.

fibre optics noun

Fibre optics is the technology of sending light through thin, flexible glass fibres. The light remains inside the fibre by reflecting off the inside of its surface. Fibre optic cables are used in telecommunications.

Fibre optic lamp.

F

filament noun

A filament is a thin thread or wire. The thin wire inside a light bulb is called a filament. When an electric **current** passes through it, it becomes white hot and therefore gives off light.

filament

filter verb

To filter is to separate solids from a liquid by straining them through material such as paper, sand or charcoal which allows liquids and air to pass through.

filtration noun This is the process of filtering.

filter noun A filter is any piece of equipment or material that can be used for filtration.

filter paper noun

A filter paper is a sheet of paper that allows liquids or gases to pass through, but stops most solid particles.

Filter paper being used to separate liquid from insoluble solids.

fish noun

Fish are **cold-blooded**, **vertebrate** (back-boned) animals that live in water. Most fish have streamlined (smooth-shaped) bodies, fins and a tail to help them swim. They have organs called gills, which allow them to absorb oxygen from water. Sharks, salmon, and plaice are some types of fish.

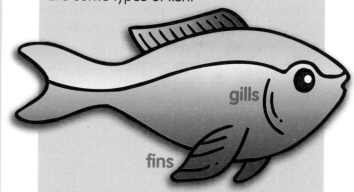

gills

fins

flame noun

Flames are tongue-shaped areas of glowing gas that form when fuel is burned.

flammable adjective

If a material is flammable it can catch fire easily: for example, oil. Flammable and inflammable mean the same thing: non-flammable is the opposite of flammable.

flexible adjective

A flexible material is one that we can bend or stretch. The opposite is rigid or inflexible.

float verb

An object floats if it stops on or near the surface of a liquid, or rises towards the surface. Light objects, like balloons, can also float in a **gas**, such as air. The opposite of float is sink.

See also: **buoyant**, **upthrust**.

flower noun

In flowering plants the flower is where the **reproductive** parts are found (the parts that are used to create a new plant). **Pollen** from the same or a different plant **fertilizes** the female parts of the flower to produce the **seeds**, which grow into new plants.

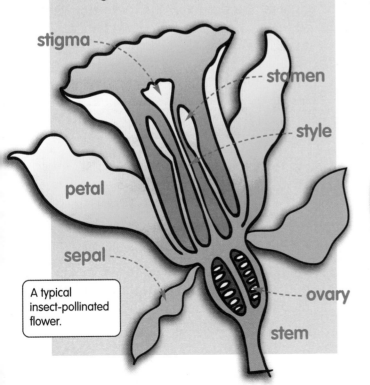

stigma

stamen

style

petal

sepal

ovary

A typical insect-pollinated flower.

stem

fluid noun

Materials that flow (liquids and gases) are fluids. Unlike solids, they do not have a particular shape; they take the shape of the container in which they are placed.

fluoride noun

Fluoride is a chemical that helps to prevent tooth decay. It is sometimes added to water supplies and put into toothpaste.

foetus noun

(pronounced 'feetus')
Between 8 weeks old and birth, a baby developing in the mother's womb is called a foetus; before 8 weeks it is called an **embryo**.

food chain noun

Food chains are ways of showing feeding relationships between living things. They are usually presented as diagrams with arrows. Each arrow means 'is food for' or 'is eaten by'.

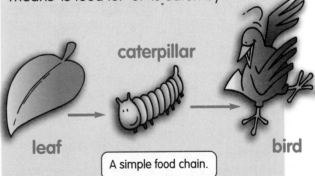

caterpillar

leaf

bird

A simple food chain.

See also: **consumer**, **predator**, **prey**, **producer**.

F

force noun

The power which makes things start and stop, change speed or direction, or change shape, is a force. Pushes and pulls are forces, but there are other forces too, such as gravity, friction, magnetism and electricity.

Forces are measured in newtons (N).

force meter noun

A force meter is an instrument for measuring forces. A simple force meter is a spring that stretches when it is pulled. This moves a pointer along a scale, measuring the force of the pull.

Force meters are marked in newtons, the standard unit of force.

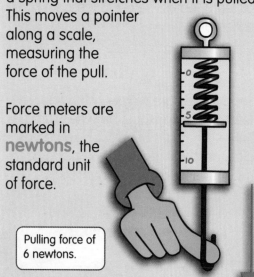

Pulling force of 6 newtons.

forensic science noun

This is the study of science in connection with the law, for example in investigating crime. People who do this job are called forensic scientists.

formula noun

(plural: formulae or formulas)
In chemistry (the study of materials and their properties) formulae are used as a quick way of writing down the names of different chemicals.

A chemical formula also tells us what parts (atoms) a chemical is made of. A water particle, for example, has two hydrogen atoms and one oxygen atom, so its formula is H_2O. Carbon dioxide has one carbon atom and two oxygen atoms, so its formula is CO_2.

fossil noun

The hardened remains of an animal or plant that are often encased in rock. Fossils provide us with clues about what life on Earth was like in prehistoric times.

Some animals and plants that died millions of years ago left only a trace or print on the surface of the rocks that were forming. These prints are called trace fossils.

fossilize verb This means to turn into a fossil.

Fossil fish.

fossil fuel noun Some prehistoric animals and plants rotted after they died and were pressed into layers of coal or oil in the earth. These and natural gas are called fossil fuels.

freeze verb

When a liquid cools to a certain temperature, it freezes and turns solid. The temperature at which it does this is called its freezing point. The freezing point of water is 0°C (zero degrees Celsius).

See also: states of matter.

frequency noun

The frequency of something is how often it happens. The frequency of a wave (for example a sound wave or radio wave) is the number of waves that are produced per second.

friction noun

Friction is a force that resists or slows down objects when they rub against another surface. The energy lost in the slowing down turns to heat and sometimes a little sound.

Air resistance and water resistance are forms of friction, caused by an object moving through air or water.

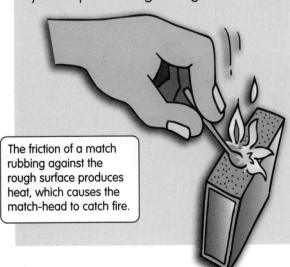

The friction of a match rubbing against the rough surface produces heat, which causes the match-head to catch fire.

fruit noun

After fertilization, the ovary of a flowering plant ripens into a fruit containing the seeds. A fruit is often soft and fleshy, for example a plum, but it can also be very hard, for example a hazelnut with its hard outer shell.

Many fruits are eaten for food, including the fruits of plants we commonly call vegetables, such as cucumbers and marrows.

fuel noun

A fuel is any material which can be burned or used up to produce energy. Wood, coal, petrol (made from oil) and natural gas are fuels. Food is the fuel that our bodies digest and turn into energy.

See also: combustion, nutrient.

F

fulcrum noun

A **lever** is a simple machine which has an arm, and a fulcrum on which it rests. The fulcrum is the point that remains still, as the rest of the machine moves. A see-saw is a kind of lever. The fulcrum is the turning point or pivot where it balances.

fulcrum

fungus noun

(plural: **fungi**)
Mushrooms, toadstools, **yeast**, moulds and **mildew** all belong to the group of living things called fungi.

A group of toadstools.

fuse noun

A fuse is a thin piece of wire in an electrical **circuit** which becomes very hot and breaks (or 'blows') if the current is too great. This breaks the circuit and stops the current; so it is a safety device.

fuse

A three-pin plug.

galaxy noun

A galaxy is a very large cluster of stars. Our Sun is one of the stars in the **Milky Way** galaxy, which contains billions of other stars.

This spiral galaxy is very similar in size and shape to our own galaxy, the Milky Way.

gas noun

Gas is matter (material) that flows freely in all directions and takes the shape of whatever container it is in. The **air** around us is a mixture of gases, including **oxygen**, **nitrogen** and **carbon dioxide**.

Gas is one of three **states of matter**. The others are **liquid** and **solid**. When a liquid **evaporates** it becomes a gas.

Many gases are **flammable** and burn when ignited (lit). Natural gas (which is also called methane) is a **fossil fuel** that is trapped underground. It is brought to the surface and supplied to homes and factories for heating and cooking.

See also: **states of matter**.

gene noun

Genes are pieces of information inside the sperm and egg cells about the characteristics (such as the colour of hair or eyes) of every living thing. They are passed down to the next **generation** when animals and plants **reproduce**. The study of **genetics** tells us that we **inherit** (take) genes from our parents, and this is why we resemble our parents in certain ways.

generation noun

A generation is the time it takes for a group of humans or other animals to mature (become fully grown) and have young of their own.

Brothers, sisters and cousins can belong to the same generation and their sons and daughters will belong to the next generation. Parents, uncles and aunts belong to the previous generation.

Generation 1 - grandparents.

Generation 2 - parents.

Generation 3 - children.

generator noun

A generator is a machine that converts rapid movement into electrical energy. A wire coil is made to rotate (go round) between magnets, and this produces an electrical current in the wire.

genetic engineering noun

Altering the **genes** to make changes in a **species** (group of living things) is called 'genetic engineering'. For example, genetically-modified (GM) crops are produced when the genes in plants are altered, for example to make them resistant to diseases.

genetics noun

Genetics is the science or study of **genes** and of inheritance.

See also: **inherit**.

geography noun

Geography is the study of the world we live in, including its physical characteristics (for example, mountains, rivers, forests), its climate, its countries and cities, its people, and the way they live.

geology noun

Geology is the study of rocks on and below the Earth's surface. It includes the study of **volcanoes** and **earthquakes**.

germ noun

Germs are tiny, living things that cause illnesses. Harmful **bacteria** and **viruses** are examples of germs.

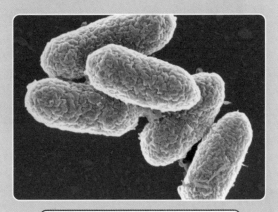

Magnified salmonella bacteria. These germs are the most common cause of food poisoning in humans.

germinate verb

Seeds germinate when they start to sprout and produce new plants.

germination noun
Germination is the name of the process by which a seed grows and develops. Moisture and warmth help germination.

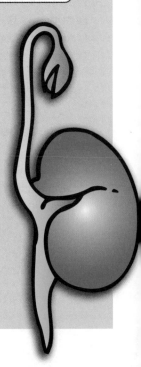

A bean at the time of germination.

gestation noun

Gestation (pregnancy) is the time between when an **embryo** forms in the **womb** of a female animal and the birth of the baby (9 months in humans; between 20–22 months in elephants).

Elephant	510 - 730 days
Human	270 days
Pig	101 - 130 days
Cat	52 - 69 days
Fox	51 - 63 days
Mouse	20 days

Table showing gestation periods of a variety of animals.

gibbous adjective

This means rounded or bulging, like the Moon just before and after it is full.

See also: **phases of the Moon.**

A gibbous moon.

gills plural noun

See **fish**.

gland noun

A gland is an organ in the body which produces a substance such as a **digestive** juice or a **hormone**.

glass noun

Glass is a hard, **transparent** or **translucent** material, made by cooling molten sand. (Molten sand is sand that has been made into liquid by great heat.)

global warming noun

Many scientists are worried that the Earth's average temperature is gradually rising. This effect is called global warming and is caused by the **greenhouse effect**. It could cause the ice at the North and South Poles to melt and the sea level to rise.

granite noun

Granite is a hard **igneous** rock.

G

graph noun

A graph is a diagram that records information or measurements. Scientists use graphs to show patterns in data (information). Different types of graph are shown below.

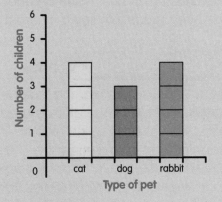

Block graph to show the number of children who have cats, dogs and rabbits in Class 2.

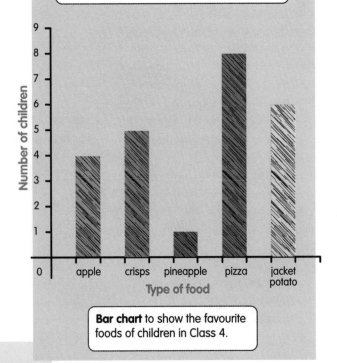

Bar chart to show the favourite foods of children in Class 4.

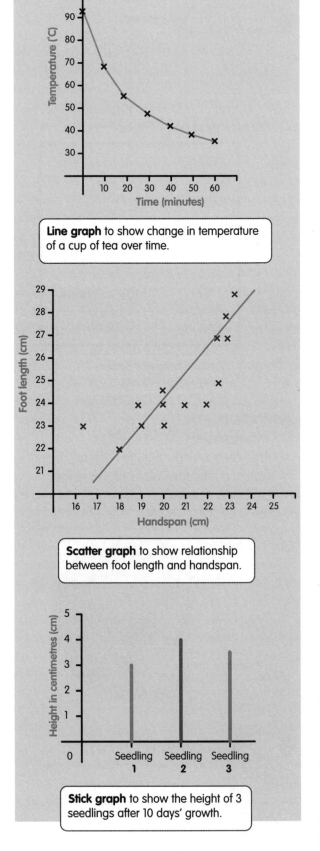

Line graph to show change in temperature of a cup of tea over time.

Scatter graph to show relationship between foot length and handspan.

Stick graph to show the height of 3 seedlings after 10 days' growth.

gravity noun

Gravity is an invisible **force** of **attraction** that pulls objects towards each other. Objects on or above the Earth's surface have weight because gravity pulls them down towards the centre of the planet.

As the Moon is smaller than the Earth, its gravity is weaker. Objects on the Moon feel lighter than they do on the Earth. Gravity has an effect over large distances. The Sun's pull on the Earth and the other planets keeps them in their **orbits**. Without gravity they would fly off into space.

Gravity was first explained by Sir Isaac Newton in the 17th century.

See also: **Earth**, **force**, **Moon**, **tide**, **weight**.

An astronaut can jump higher on the Moon than on Earth because gravity on the Moon is $\frac{1}{6}$ of that on the Earth.

greenhouse effect noun

The glass sides and roof of a greenhouse let in sunlight, which warms up the air and the objects inside, but the glass does not let the heat escape, so the temperature rises. The Earth and its atmosphere are like a giant greenhouse: **carbon dioxide** and water vapour trap the Sun's heat, and this causes the Earth and its atmosphere to warm up.

The burning of fossil fuels (such as oil, petrol and coal) increases the amount of carbon dioxide in the atmosphere, so making the greenhouse effect greater. The result is **global warming**.

gut noun

See **intestine**.

H

habitat noun

A habitat is the place or area where a creature or plant lives. For example, the natural habitat of a squirrel is woodland.

haemophilia noun

(pronounced heemo-feelia)
Haemophilia is a disease that prevents blood from clotting (forming into a thick mass). Clotting stops bleeding, so a person with haemophilia has to be careful all the time not to get cut or bruised. Haemophilia is the first disease that was found to be passed on from one generation to the next.

heart noun

The heart is a powerful muscular organ in humans and many other animals that pumps blood around the body.

heartbeat noun The heart pumps the blood by contracting (or squeezing). Each squeeze is called a heartbeat and sends a pulse of blood through the arteries (tubes which carry blood away from the heart). Veins bring blood back to the heart.

See also: circulatory system.

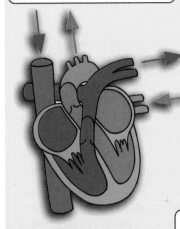

Blood flows around the body and back to the heart.

Blood goes to the lungs to collect oxygen, and returns to the heart.

A human heart.

helium noun

Helium is a gas that is lighter than air. Balloons filled with helium weigh less than the same amount of air, so the balloon rises or floats.

See also: gas and density.

Helium-filled balloon.

hemisphere   noun

Hemisphere means 'half a sphere'. The Earth is a sphere: one half is called the northern hemisphere and the other the southern hemisphere.

See also: season.

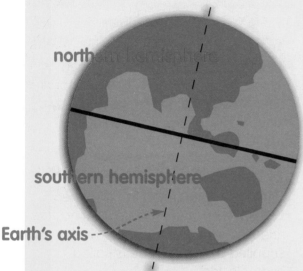

northern hemisphere

southern hemisphere

Earth's axis

herbivore   noun

A herbivore is an animal that eats only plant food.

See also: carnivore, omnivore.

heredity   noun

Heredity is the taking on of characteristics (such as green eyes and red hair) from our parents or grandparents.

hereditary adjective Something that has been passed down from one generation to another, through the genes, is described as hereditary.

hibernate   verb

Animals that hibernate hide away and sleep, or become inactive, during the winter months. Some of the animals that hibernate are dormice, frogs, bats, and hedgehogs. Animals hibernate to save energy during a time of year when it is difficult for them to find energy-giving food.

hinge joint   noun

Joints are points in the skeleton where bones can move in relation to one another to allow the body to move. Hinge joints work like the ordinary hinges that we use on doors: they allow movement only in one direction and back. The human elbow and knee are hinge joints.

See also: ball and socket joint.

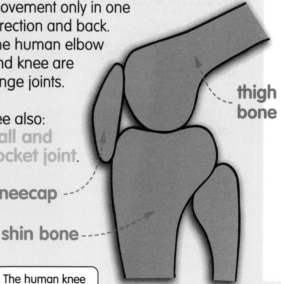

thigh bone

kneecap

shin bone

The human knee has a hinge joint.

H

hologram noun

A hologram is a 3-dimensional image. It is made by burning a picture into the surface of a material that reflects light. The pattern of light waves reflecting off the surface creates the image.

horizon noun

The furthest points that you can see on the Earth's surface lie on the horizon. It is the line where the sky and the Earth appear to meet.

hormone noun

Chemicals produced by glands (organs) in the body which control growth and changes to the body. For example, the changes that occur at puberty are controlled by hormones. There are some differences between the hormones that males and females have.

humidity noun

Humidity is the amount of water vapour in the air. If the weather is very humid, it feels damp. Humidity is caused by evaporation.

See also: hygrometer.

humus noun

Humus is the dark-coloured remains of decayed plants and animals that mixes with particles of rock, to make up the soil. It supplies new plants with many nutrients and helps soil to hold water.

hydraulic adjective

Anything that is driven by water, or other liquid under pressure, is described as hydraulic. For example, hydraulic brakes are connected to the brake pedal by a tube filled with pressurized liquid.

hydroelectric power noun

Electricity is generated (made) when a turbine is driven by water that has been released from a dam. The power supplied by this method is called hydroelectric.

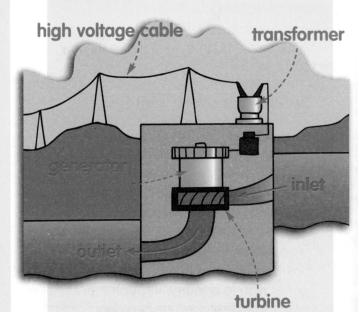

high voltage cable   transformer

generator   inlet

outlet

turbine

hydrogen   noun

Hydrogen is a gas. It has no colour and no smell, and is highly flammable. It is the least dense of all materials, and therefore much lighter than air. Like helium it can be used to fill balloons, but is unsuitable because of the danger of fire.

The Hindenburg was a hydrogen-filled airship, which caught fire and exploded in 1937.

hygrometer   noun

A hygrometer is an instrument used to measure humidity in the air.

hypothesis   noun

(plural: hypotheses, pronounced hypotha-seez)
A hypothesis is like a prediction. Scientists work by making hypotheses (or statements that they think are true). They then test their statements to see whether they are right or wrong.

400 years ago Galileo made the hypothesis that a stone and a feather would fall at the same speed if there were no air resistance, for example, on the Moon. Scientific experiments and observations have since proved his hypothesis correct.

Gee!
Galileo was right!

ice noun

Ice is water that has frozen and become solid. Ice is one of the three states in which water can exist. The other two are liquid and gas (water vapour).

See also: states of matter.

igneous rock noun

Molten material from inside the Earth, which has cooled and become solid rock is called igneous rock.

Igneous rocks are usually crystalline.

Basalt.

Granite.

image noun

An image is something that we see as a result of light reflecting from an object into our eyes.

immune adjective

If we are immune to a disease, it means we can fight it without becoming ill; we do not get all the symptoms (signs) of the disease. Medicines called vaccines can immunize us against some diseases; they prompt our body's defences, so they react more quickly the next time our body comes into contact with the disease.

If the body's immune system is damaged, for example by the HIV virus, it can no longer fight disease as effectively.

incisor noun

See teeth.

incubate verb

An egg is incubated (kept warm) until it hatches (until a young bird or reptile emerges from it). This is necessary for the embryo to develop inside the egg. Birds sit on their eggs, so that their body heat can be used for incubation.

incubator noun A heated box used to incubate eggs and other living things during early stages of development.

infection noun

Infection is caused by germs (bacteria, viruses, and fungi) invading the body. A wound can become infected when dirt containing germs gets into it.

A disease is infectious if it can be spread from one person, or other living thing, to another.

Disinfectants can be used to prevent or fight infection by killing germs.

infrared adjective

See electromagnetic spectrum.

inhale verb

To inhale is to take air into the lungs. The lungs expand as they fill with air. The opposite is exhale.

inhaler noun

An inhaler is a device that sprays medicine (in the form of vapour) into the nose or throat to help with breathing. It is helpful to people who are affected by asthma.

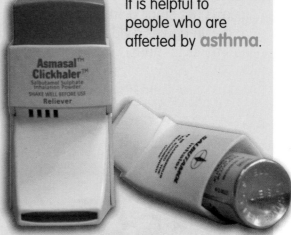

A range of inhalers is available on prescription from a doctor.

inherit verb

To inherit is to take on the characteristics of our parents, for example eye colour or hair colour.

inoculate verb

Inoculate means to introduce a virus or bacterium into the body of a person or animal, for example, to vaccinate them.

See also: immune.

I

inorganic adjective

Something that is not alive, and has never been alive, is called inorganic. It is the opposite of organic.

insect noun

Insects are small animals with six legs and with bodies divided into three main segments (or parts).

Insects are invertebrates.

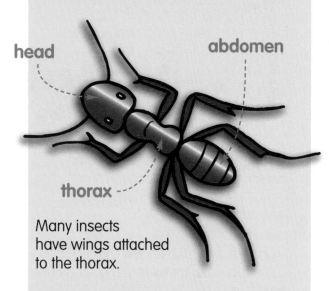

head

abdomen

thorax

Many insects have wings attached to the thorax.

insoluble adjective

If a material is insoluble in water, this means that it will not dissolve in it.

The opposite is soluble.

insulator noun

An insulator is a material through which heat, sound or electricity does not travel. It is the opposite of a conductor. For example, wool insulates our bodies well, preventing us from losing heat. Bare electric wires are covered with a layer of plastic to insulate them. Padded walls or double-glazing on windows provide some insulation against noise.

intestines plural noun

Intestines are the tubes inside the body through which food passes during digestion (when chemicals inside the body break down the food, so that the nutrients can be used). There are two sections of intestine, the large and the small, starting from the stomach and finishing at the anus.

The intestines are also called 'the guts' or 'the gut'.

See also: digestive system.

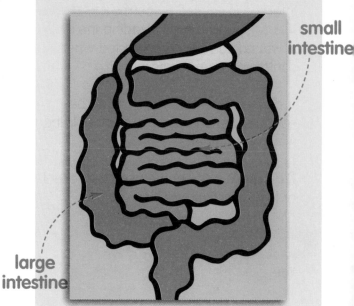

small intestine

large intestine

invertebrate · noun

An invertebrate is an animal that has no backbone inside its body to support it.

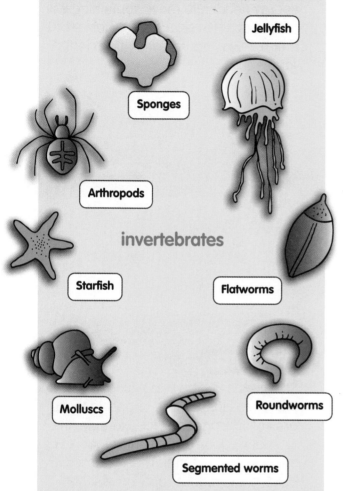

Jellyfish

Sponges

Arthropods

invertebrates

Starfish

Flatworms

Molluscs

Roundworms

Segmented worms

investigation · noun

Investigation means finding out. In a scientific investigation observations and tests are used to find out how and why things happen, what living and non-living things are made of and how they work.

investigate verb To carry out an investigation.

ion · noun

An ion is an atom (or collection of atoms) that has an electric charge (electricity contained inside it) because it has gained or lost electrons. Electrons have a negative charge, so losing electrons makes an atom into a positive ion; gaining electrons makes it a negative ion.

irreversible change · noun

When materials are mixed, heated, and burned, new materials are made. Changes have taken place. Some of these changes are irreversible, which means the new material(s) cannot be made back into the original one(s).

For example, when a piece of wood is burned, an irreversible chemical change takes place. The wood and some oxygen in the air react (mix together and change) to make soot and smoke and gases. This change cannot be reversed; the wood cannot be remade.

See also: reversible change.

J

joint noun

A joint is a place in the **skeleton** where bones are joined together to allow movement.

See **ball and socket joint** and **hinge joint**.

joule noun

A joule is the standard unit used to measure energy. One joule is roughly the energy needed to move something using a force of 1 **newton** for a distance of 1 metre. It was named after the scientist, James Joule.

K

key noun

A key is a chart that can be used to identify individual members of a group by listing **characteristics**. For example, there are keys that identify different insects by their size, colouring, whether or not they have wings etc.

kingdom noun

Scientists describe living things by sorting them into classes. The largest of these are called kingdoms: for example, the animal kingdom, the plant kingdom, and the kingdom of fungi. These classes are divided into smaller and smaller sub-classes, the smallest of which are **species**.

larva noun

(the plural is **larvae**, pronounced lar-vee)

A larva is the short, worm-like form in which insects begin life, before they change into their adult form.

See also: **metamorphosis**.

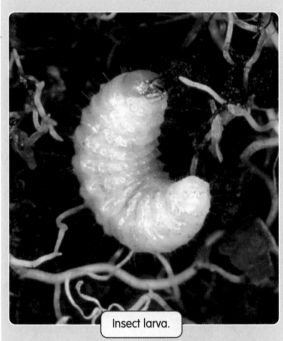

Insect larva.

lava noun

Lava is molten rock that flows from a **volcano**

LCD abbreviation

LCD is short for Liquid Crystal Display. The liquid is contained between two sheets of glass, and becomes visible when a small electrical **voltage** is applied to it. Many electronic devices have LCDs, for example pocket calculators.

LED abbreviation

An LED is a device called a diode that gives out light when a small electrical **voltage** is applied to it. (A diode is a component that allows the flow of electricity in one direction but does not allow it in the other.) The letters stand for Light Emitting Diode. LEDs are used for many digital displays, for example on car stereos or radios.

L

lens noun

A lens is a piece of glass, or other transparent material, with curved surfaces. Because light slows down when it travels into the glass, the beams change direction slightly. The lens is shaped to bend the light beams, so that they converge (come together) or diverge (move apart). This makes images seen through a lens look larger or smaller than they really are.

The **eyes** of humans and other animals contain lenses which focus light. Cameras, microscopes, telescopes and binoculars are fitted with lenses for the same purpose.

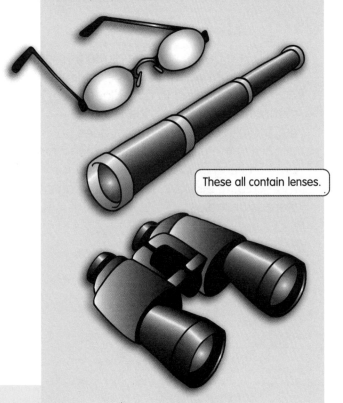

These all contain lenses.

leukaemia noun

(pronounced loo-keemia)
Leukaemia is a serious illness that affects the white blood cells. It can be, but is not always, fatal (meaning people can die from it).

lever noun

A lever is a simple mechanism, consisting of a strong bar, called the arm, and a fixed point for the arm to move against. The fixed point is called a pivot, or **fulcrum**.

If the fulcrum is nearer to one end of the lever than the other, work, such as lifting something heavy, or opening a tight-fitting lid, is made easier.

pivot

effort

lichen noun

(pronounced lye-ken or litchin)
Lichen is a crusty, scaly plant-growth found on trees and on rocks.

life cycle noun

All living things begin life and can grow, mature, become old, and die. They can also **reproduce** (make young), so that new life begins. This process is called a **cycle**, because it keeps repeating.

See also: **metamorphosis**, **pollination**.

baby: 0-1 year

embryo in humans: 9 months

child: 1-11 years

adolescent: 11-18 years

adulthood: 18-65 years

old age: 65+ years

life processes plural noun

The following are the processes which show that something is alive; therefore they are called the life processes.
- move
- grow
- feed: take in nutrients and convert them into energy
- breathe (or respire): take in oxygen and use it to convert food into energy
- excrete: get rid of waste
- sense: see, feel, hear, smell, taste
- reproduce: produce new living things; have young.

ligament noun

Ligaments are tough strands or cords that connect bones to each other.

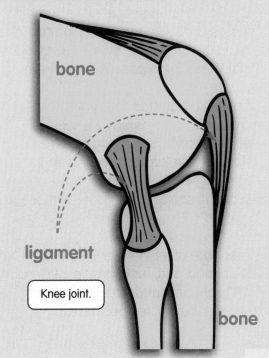

bone

ligament

Knee joint.

bone

L

light noun

Light is a form of radiation that comes from very hot burning material, for example from the Sun and other stars. Light can be natural (such as that which comes from the Sun, stars and lightning) and artificial (such as the light from electric bulbs, torches and candles). Some animals also give out light; for example, glow worms and angler fish.

Light travels in straight beams through empty space, at a speed of approximately 300 000 km per second. At this speed light from the Sun takes around 7 minutes to reach the Earth.

Light passes through transparent materials, such as air, water, glass, clear plastic. Other materials allow some light to pass through and reflect the rest; they are translucent. Opaque materials allow no light to pass through them.

Light radiation has different wavelengths, which we see as different colours, ranging from red to violet. These form what is called the visible spectrum. White light, such as sunlight, contains a mixture of these colours.

There are other wavelengths of light that we cannot see, for example ultra-violet (UV) light and infrared light. They are outside the visible spectrum.

UV light is contained in sunlight. It can damage skin and eyes. Humans can protect themselves by using protective sun cream and wearing sunglasses that filter out harmful UV light rays.

See also: electromagnetic spectrum.

A rainbow forms when raindrops split sunlight up into the colours of the visible spectrum.

lightning noun

Lightning is a massive electric spark. It happens when rain and ice particles rub together in a cloud, causing electricity to build up. The electricity then discharges (escapes) by leaping across the gap to another cloud or to the Earth.

This causes a sudden, bright flash of light and a loud crack, which echoes for miles around producing the rumbling noise of thunder.

Lightning striking a city in Arizona, USA.

limestone noun

Limestone is a rock with a smooth, pale surface. It is a **sedimentary** rock, sometimes containing shells and coral (a hard substance made of the skeletons of tiny sea creatures) that have settled on the sea bed and hardened under pressure into rock.

Limestone is ground into powder called irhe; this is used in making cement and also as a **fertilizer** by farmers, since it balances the **acid** in soil.

Shelly limestone.

liquid adjective and noun

One of the **states of matter** in which materials can be found is liquid. Liquids flow and take the shape of whatever container they are in.

At room temperature water is a liquid, but it becomes a **solid** when it freezes and it becomes a **gas** when it **evaporates**.

See also: **states of matter**.

liverwort noun

Liverworts are green, non-flowering plants similar to **moss**. They grow on rocks, logs, or damp earth, and were one of the first plants in the history of the Earth to grow on land.

Liverwort.

lubricant noun

A lubricant is a material, such as oil or grease, which reduces the **friction** between two surfaces. **Lubricating** the moving parts of a machine allows them to work more smoothly, and stops them wearing out quickly.

luminous adjective

A luminous object is one that radiates light. A light bulb is luminous when it has been switched on. The Sun is also luminous, but the Moon is not, since it is only visible because it reflects the light of the Sun.

L

lunar adjective

Lunar means to do with the Moon. For example, a lunar eclipse is an eclipse of the Moon.

lungs plural noun

The lungs are the organs that humans and other animals use for breathing (respiration). The lungs are protected by bones, which form the rib-cage.

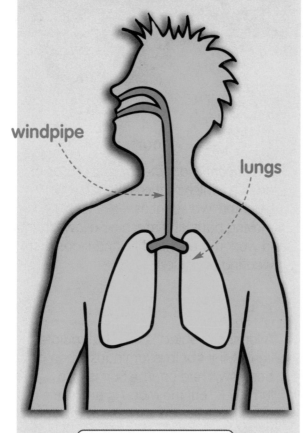

windpipe

lungs

Position of lungs in the body.

magnet · noun

A magnet is an object which **attracts** anything made of, or containing, iron, for example, steel. The opposite ends of a magnet are called **poles**: a north pole and a south pole. If the north and south poles of two separate magnets are brought close together, they attract each other. If like poles (e.g. a north and another north) are brought close together they **repel** each other.

Opposite poles attract

Like poles repel

Like poles repel

magnetic field · noun

Magnets are surrounded by a region called a magnetic field. The effect of the magnet can be felt anywhere in the field.

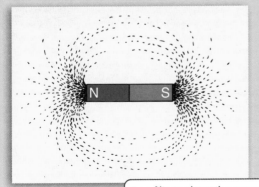

Iron filings show the magnetic field around a bar magnet.

magnetism · noun

Magnetism is a **force** that magnets exert, or the effect they have on materials.

Objects that are magnets, or are attracted by magnets, are described as **magnetic** materials.

magnify · verb

Magnifying something means making it look larger, for example, with a lens.

malnutrition noun

Someone suffering from malnutrition has had too little food, or the wrong kind of food, to stay healthy.

mammal noun

Mammal is a class of animal that includes humans, cats, rabbits, etc. Mammals are **vertebrates**. They are **warm-blooded** and have a covering of body hair; the females produce milk on which they feed their young.

Most mammals give birth to live babies, but platypuses and spiny ant-eaters are mammals that lay eggs.

Whales and dolphins are marine mammals, or aquatic mammals (meaning sea- or water-mammals).

Mammals.

manufactured adjective

An object or material which is manufactured has been made by humans or machines.

marble noun

Marble is a rock (a form of **limestone**). Like limestone it is high in **calcium**, as it was formed from the shells and bones of sea-creatures. But unlike limestone, marble is a **metamorphic** rock, which means that heat and pressure changed it into a dense, **crystalline** rock.

Marble is valued for its beauty, its many different colours, and the fact that it can be polished to give it a smooth, shiny surface.

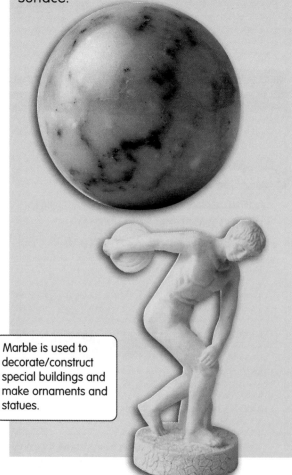

Marble is used to decorate/construct special buildings and make ornaments and statues.

marine life (noun)

Marine life is life in the sea.

mass (noun)

Mass is the amount of **matter** out of which something is made. Mass is not the same as size: a brick is a lot more **massive** than a piece of polystyrene foam that has been cut to the same size. The standard unit for measuring mass is grams/kilograms.

The more mass an object has, the more it weighs. However, weight also depends on gravity. On the Moon, where gravity is weaker, a 1 kg object would weigh a lot less than it does on Earth; but it still has a mass of 1 kg.

See also: **weight**, **gravity**.

material (noun)

The different kinds of **matter** that things are made of are called materials. Wool, metal, oil and air are examples of materials.

Some materials, such as glass and plastic, are man-made from other materials. Others, such as wood, rock and sand are **natural**.

The properties of materials are what make them different from each other: whether they are hard, smooth, absorbent, elastic, transparent, etc. There are also different **states** that materials can be in: **gas**, **liquid**, **solid**.

See also: **states of matter**.

matter (noun)

Matter is the scientific word for the material out of which all objects and materials are made.

The stars, planets, and everything on them, are matter, right down to the smallest **atom**.

mature (adjective)

A living thing that is fully grown, or has become adult, is mature. The opposite is immature.

medicine (noun)

A medicine is anything that is taken to improve a person's health, or to cure or help someone who is unwell or in pain (for example Paracetamol liquid). **Drugs** are medicines when they are used in this way.

Medicines for headaches, colds, cuts and bruises, etc. can be bought in a pharmacy (chemist's shop). Special or more powerful medicines need a **prescription** from a doctor.

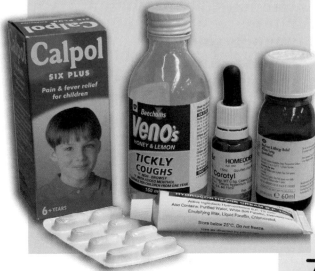

melanin noun

Melanin is a natural, dark **pigment** (a substance that gives colour to something). It is found in skin and hair and eyes. It helps to protect our skin from sunlight and **radiation**.

Darker skin and hair contain larger amounts of the pigment called melanin.

melt verb

Solid materials melt, and become **liquid** when they reach a certain temperature.

See also: **states of matter**.

melting point noun

The melting point of a material is the temperature at which it changes from a solid state into a liquid one. The melting point of water (ice) is 0 °C (zero degrees Celsius). Rock does not melt (or become **molten**) below around 1000 °C (one thousand degrees Celsius).

menstrual cycle noun

The regularly-repeated monthly pattern of changes that take place in the reproductive organs of mature females. An egg is produced each month. The lining of the **womb** thickens in preparation for **fertilization** of the egg. If this does not occur, the lining of the womb is shed (breaks down).

See also: **menstrual period**, **reproduction**.

menstrual period noun

A time span of 3–7 days, during each month, when the lining of the **womb** of sexually-mature human females and apes, breaks down and passes out of the **vagina**. During this time a female is often said to be 'having her period'. Periods normally stop during pregnancy (when a female is carrying a baby inside her).

metal noun

Most metals are hard, strong materials which are good **conductors** of heat and electricity. Copper, iron, steel, tin, zinc, gold, silver, platinum and lead, are all examples of metals.

Pure metals can be mixed to form **alloys**.

metamorphic rock (noun)

Metamorphic rocks are those whose properties were changed by tremendous heat and pressure when they were formed, for example, slate and marble.

Marble - a good material for buildings and statues.

metamorphosis (noun)

A metamorphosis is a change. In particular it means the process by which a **larva** changes into an adult insect.

metamorphose verb This means to change. For example, a caterpillar metamorphoses into a butterfly.

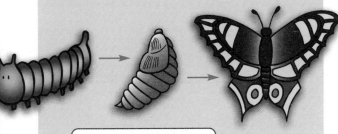

The life cycle of a butterfly.

meteor (noun)

A meteor (also called a 'shooting star') is the bright streak of light caused when an object (a **meteoroid**) falls from out in space towards the Earth. **Friction** against the atmosphere makes a meteor glow brightly before it burns and turns to **vapour**.

Most meteoroids are small and never reach the Earth. (Some are no bigger than grains of sand.) Those that reach the ground are called **meteorites**. Some meteorites are so massive that they make large craters in the earth.

Crater made by a meteorite in Arizona, USA about 50,000 years ago. It is 200 metres deep and 800 metres across.

meteorology noun

Meteorology is the study of weather, or of anything to do with the **atmosphere**.

micro- prefix

Words to do with being very small often begin with 'micro–', for example microscope, and micro-organism.

microbe noun

Microbes, (or micro-organisms) are living things. Single microbes are too small to be seen without the help of a microscope, but in groups or colonies they are visible to the naked eye. Microbes include organisms such as **fungi**, **bacteria**, and **viruses**. Some microbes are harmful to animals and plants because they cause infections and disease, but there are others that are very useful: for example, in rotting waste materials; or in making yoghurt, cheese, bread, wine and beer, and in **antibiotics**, which fight bacterial infections.

micro-organism noun

See: **microbe**.

microprocessor noun

A microprocessor is the very complex but tiny set of electric circuits that process data inside computers.

microscope noun

A microscope is an instrument that magnifies small objects, so that they can be seen more clearly.

microscopic adjective Something that is microscopic is too small to be seen without a microscope.

mildew noun

This is a type of **fungus** that can grow on leaves, clothes, paper etc., especially when they are damp.

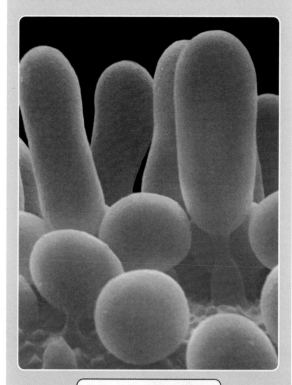

Magnified mildew spores.

Milky Way noun

This is the name given to the galaxy, (or large cluster of stars) of which the Earth and Sun are a part. The Milky Way consists of billions of stars.

The billions of stars in the Milky Way form a band of light in the night sky.

mineral noun

A mineral is any natural, but non-living (**inorganic**) material, such as metals and crystalline substances. Small amounts of some minerals are essential parts of the diet of humans and other animals, for example salt and iron. Plants also need minerals; they take these from the soil.

Crystals of a mineral.

mirror noun

A mirror is a smooth, shiny surface that reflects light.

The surface of a mirror can be flat or curved. A flat mirror reflects an image that is true to life (but the left and the right sides have been reversed). A curved mirror changes the shape and size of the image by reflecting light beams in different directions.

See also: **reflection**.

mixture noun

When two or more materials are put together in a container they can form a mixture. Solids, like sand and soil, can be mixed. So can two or more liquids, or liquids and solids, for example salt and water. If a solid dissolves in a liquid, the mixture is called a **solution**.

Some mixtures can be sieved or filtered to separate the materials in them. Solutions can be evaporated to separate the solids from the liquid.

Some mixtures result in **irreversible changes/chemical changes** to the materials, so that they cannot be separated afterwards.

molar noun

See **teeth**.

molecule noun

If two or more **atoms** join together they form a molecule. The atoms can be the same kind, or different kinds. An oxygen molecule has two oxygen atoms. A carbon dioxide molecule has two oxygen atoms and one carbon atom.

A water molecule has two hydrogen atoms and one oxygen atom.

molten adjective

When a solid, such as rock or iron, is heated up to its **melting point** and turns to liquid, it becomes molten.

moon noun

A moon is a natural **satellite** that orbits (circles) a planet. The planet Jupiter has 16 known moons. The Earth has one natural satellite, known as the Moon.

Moon noun The Moon is a small planet that orbits (circles) the Earth. It does not give out any light of its own, but it shows up brightly at night because it reflects light from the Sun.

See also: **phases of the Moon**.

moss noun

Mosses are green, non-flowering plants that grow on stones, trees, and damp earth. Mosses and **liverworts** are two of the oldest plants in the history of the Earth to grow on land.

motor noun

A motor is a machine that produces movement. An electric motor, for example, uses electromagnetic forces to turn an arm inside it (called a rotor).

mould noun

Mould is a **fungus** that can grow on decaying food, or on plants or wood.

mouldy adjective Something with mould growing on it is described as mouldy.

Mouldy bread.

muscle noun

Muscles are bands of fibres (very thin threads) in the body that produce different movements. Some muscles are attached to bones. They work by **contracting**, so that they pull. This causes the skeleton to move. To produce the opposite movement the muscle has to relax (loosen), whilst another muscle contracts.

Some muscles are called 'voluntary'. They contract when we want to do something, such as raise an arm. Other muscles are 'involuntary', and work by themselves. The heart, which pumps the blood round the body, is an involuntary muscle.

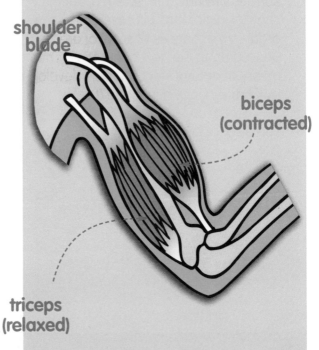

shoulder blade

biceps (contracted)

triceps (relaxed)

natural adjective

A natural material or object is one that is found in nature, and not made by humans.

natural selection noun

According to the theory of natural selection the creatures and plants that survive and reproduce are the ones that are best suited to their surroundings (or environment). Creatures and plants that do not adapt to their environment do not survive. In this way all the different species are naturally selected. The characteristics that increase an organism's chances of survival are passed on to the next generation. The theory of natural selection was developed by Charles Darwin in the 1870s.

See also: evolution.

nectar noun

Nectar is a sweet-tasting liquid that flowering plants produce to attract bees and other insects into them. Many flowering plants need to be visited by insects, so that pollination can occur. Bees collect nectar to make honey. Nectar is produced in a part of the plant called the nectary, which is usually at the base of the flower.

negative adjective

Electric charge (the amount of electrical energy stored in something) is described either as negative or positive. The terminals of a battery (the places to which wires are connected) are also called negative or positive.

positive terminal

negative terminal

nerve   noun

See nervous system.

nervous system   noun

The nervous system is the network of nerves (cords) in the body that connect the brain to the muscles and to the sense organs. The nerves carry messages and instructions to and from the brain.

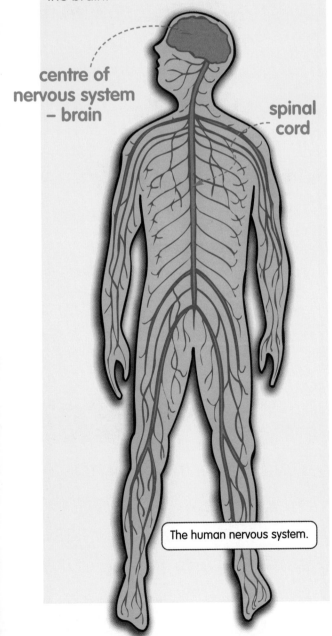

centre of nervous system – brain

spinal cord

The human nervous system.

newton   noun

A newton is the standard unit that scientists use to measure forces, such as weight. 1 newton (or 1N) is roughly equal to the weight on Earth of a 100-gram object.

See also: weight, gravity.

newton meter   noun

See force meter.

nicotine   noun

Nicotine is a poisonous substance that is found in tobacco. It is this drug that makes smoking addictive (a habit that people cannot easily stop).

nitrogen   noun

Nitrogen is a gas. It is invisible and has no smell. About 80% of the air is nitrogen.

N

nitrogen cycle noun

Nitrogen in the air makes compounds (mixes) with other materials in the soil. It is taken up by plants, which are in turn eaten by animals. The nitrogen is returned to the soil in the form of waste or decaying matter. This repeating process forms a continuous cycle.

nocturnal adjective

Animals that are active at night or flowers that open at night are classed as nocturnal.

See also: diurnal.

nucleus noun

See atom.

nutrient noun

Living things need nutrients for their life processes. Plants need water and minerals from the soil in order to grow, as well as light.

Animals need carbohydrates, fats and proteins for energy and growth. They also need minerals and vitamins for good health.

nutrition noun Nutrition is the process of taking in nutrients. It also means the scientific study of food and dietary needs.

observatory noun

An observatory is a place where **astronomers** observe and photograph planets, stars, galaxies, etc., using powerful **telescopes**.

Observatories have to be built away from bright lights and areas with high air pollution because these can distort the view of the night sky; for this reason they are often built on mountains.

Observatories in Chile. The high altitude (2300 metres) and the clear air make the site an ideal location for astronomical observations.

observe verb

When a scientist observes something, or makes an **observation**, it means more than just looking. It means carefully studying objects and events and collecting facts about them. It means using all the **senses**, and instruments such as microscopes, thermometers, etc. Observation may involve testing and measuring, to find information.

From observations scientists form **theories** and draw **conclusions**.

oesophagus noun

The oesophagus is a tube that connects the mouth to the stomach. Its job is to carry food from the mouth to the stomach.

See also: **digestive system**.

oil noun

Oils are liquids that have a slippery feel. They have many uses, for example, in cooking, as a **lubricant** (to make parts of machinery move smoothly) and as a fuel. They are also used in the production of many materials, including soap, plastic, paint, petrol and diesel.

Edible oils (oils we can eat) are produced from living things, such as sunflowers, olives, rape and fish. **Mineral** oils are found underground. These come from the remains of tiny plants and animals, which lived in the sea millions of years ago.

Mineral oil is highly **flammable**, especially when it has been refined to make it purer. It is used for heating, and as a fuel for cars and other vehicles.

omnivore **noun**

An omnivore is an animal that eats both meat and plants as food.

See also: carnivore, herbivore.

opaque **adjective**

If something is opaque we cannot see through it and light cannot pass through it. It is neither transparent nor translucent.

optical **adjective**

Optical means to do with sight or the eyes. For example, microscopes and telescopes that use lenses or mirrors are optical instruments.

optics **noun** This is the science of light and vision (the power to see).

optical fibre **noun**

An optical fibre is a thin, flexible strand of glass or plastic, along which light can travel by reflecting off the inside surface.

See also: fibre optics.

orbit **noun and verb**

The path through space that a planet takes around another object, such as a star, is called its orbit. The Earth takes $365\frac{1}{4}$ days (a year) to orbit the Sun. The Moon orbits the Earth once every 28 days (approximately once a month.) Planets and moons are natural satellites, but there are also many artificial satellites in orbit round the Earth.

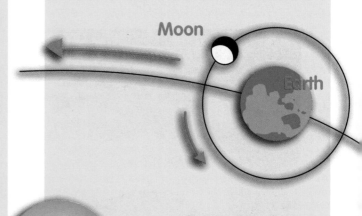

Moon

Earth

Sun

The Moon's orbit around the Earth and the Earth's orbit around the Sun.

ore **noun**

Ore is a mixture of minerals from which a pure material, such as iron or gold, can be extracted (taken out).

organ noun

Organs are parts of living things with a particular function in the body. For example, the heart is an animal organ, which pumps blood around the body. The stamen is the male reproductive organ in a flower; it produces pollen.

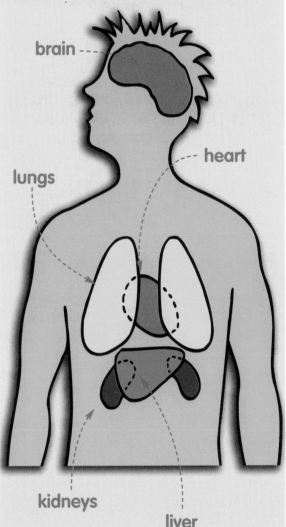

brain

heart

lungs

kidneys

liver

Some of the major organs in the human body.

organic adjective

If you call something organic, it means it is alive, or has been alive and has died. The opposite is inorganic. For example, compost from rotted plants is organic matter; but chemical fertilizer is inorganic.
The word 'organic' is often used to describe food that has been grown without using chemical fertilizers or pesticides (chemicals to kill insects and grubs).

organism noun

An organism is any living thing. Plants, animals, bacteria, and fungi are all different kinds of organism.

ovary noun

The ovary is the organ in female animals that produces the ova (eggs), which, after fertilization, become embryos. Human females have two ovaries.

In plants the ovary is the organ that produces ovules (small female parts) which, after fertilization, become seeds.

See also: flower, reproduction.

oxygen noun

Oxygen is a colourless gas with no smell or taste. Around 20% of the air that forms Earth's atmosphere is oxygen.

Oxygen (like hydrogen, nitrogen, carbon) is an element. Oxygen and hydrogen combine to form water. Oxygen and carbon together form carbon dioxide.

Oxygen is a very active material. It mixes (or reacts) with many other substances, often fiercely. Burning is a fierce reaction between oxygen and a fuel, for example wood, in the presence of heat.

Nearly all plants and animals need oxygen – even fish, which take in oxygen dissolved in water. In animals oxygen combines with food materials in the body to produce energy. Green plants take carbon dioxide from the atmosphere; they use the carbon, and return oxygen to the air.

See also: respiration, photosynthesis.

ozone noun

Ozone is a gas. It is a form of oxygen, but it is blue in colour, has a smell, and is poisonous.

Most of the ozone in the air is high in the atmosphere, in a region called the 'ozonosphere', or 'ozone layer'. The ozone layer is very useful because it absorbs harmful ultraviolet radiation from the Sun. However, air pollution is destroying some of the ozone, and making holes or thin patches in the ozone layer. This could allow radiation levels to rise dangerously high.

palaeontology noun

Palaeontology is the study of **fossil** remains and extinct life forms.

parallel circuit noun

Electrical **circuits** with two or more loops or branches are called parallel circuits. If there is a break in one loop, the current can still flow in the other loop(s).

See also: **series circuit**.

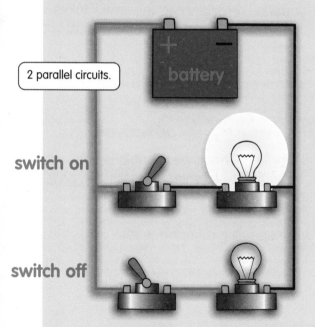

2 parallel circuits.

switch on

switch off

parasite noun

A parasite is an organism (living thing) that lives in or on another organism (called the 'host') and feeds from it, but gives nothing in return. Fleas and lice, and various kinds of worm which live in animal **intestines** are examples of parasites. Viruses are **parasitic**; so are many fungi and other plants (including mistletoe) that grow on trees.

Mistletoe is a parasitic plant.

particle noun

This word is used in a general way to mean any small, separate piece of a material: for example, a dust or sand particle.

It is also the word for the smallest units of matter: **atoms**, **molecules**, and **electrons** are particles of matter.

pasteurize verb

(or **pasteurise**)
If we pasteurize a liquid, we heat it to a high enough temperature to kill any harmful microbes that it might contain. Milk is pasteurized by heating and then rapidly cooling it. The process is named after Louis Pasteur, who discovered the effects of microbes on food, and invented the process now known as **pasteurization**.

patella noun

The patella is the flat bone at the front of the knee joint, which is also called the 'kneecap'.

P

pelvis (hip bone) noun

The pelvis is the large bone to which the spine and the leg bones are attached.

See also: skeleton.

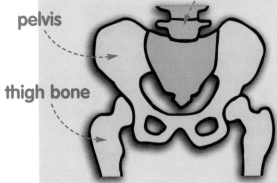

base of spine

pelvis

thigh bone

pendulum noun

A pendulum is a weight (called a 'bob') on a cord or arm that can swing freely from side to side.

Pendulums swing at a steady rate. For centuries they have been used to keep time in clocks.

penis noun

The penis is the male **reproductive organ** in humans and some other animals. **Sperm** is passed from the penis into the female's **vagina**. The penis is also used to expel urine (liquid waste).

See also: **reproduction**.

period noun

A period, in science, is the time it takes for an event to recur (or come round) in a **cycle**.

It is also short for **menstrual period**.

permeable adjective

A material that is permeable is one through which water or gases can pass. Sandstone is a permeable rock.

The opposite is impermeable.

permeability noun The property of being permeable.

petal noun

See **flower**.

petrol noun

Petrol is a highly-flammable liquid that is produced from **petroleum**. It is used as a fuel.

petroleum noun

Petroleum is a **fossil fuel**. It is a thick, oily, **flammable** liquid found underground in rocks. It is also called crude oil. It is processed (or refined) to make many products, including petrol and other fuels, and lubricating oils.

An oilrig contains machinery that can pump oil from under the ground to the surface.

pharmacology noun

Pharmacology is the science and technology of drugs that are used for medicine (the study of the way they work).

phase noun

A phase is a stage through which something goes, or the way it is at a certain time. For example, childhood is one phase that humans go through in their lifetime.

phases of the Moon plural noun

The **Moon** goes through different phases as it orbits the Earth, and the bright part that we see (lit by the Sun) changes in appearance. For about 14 days the moon appears to wax (get larger or rounder); then for 14 more days it appears to wane (get smaller and thinner).

The brightness of the Moon is caused by sunlight being reflected from its surface.

new

waxing crescent

waning crescent

first quarter

last quarter

waxing gibbous

waning gibbous

full

photosynthesis   noun

Photosynthesis is the process by which **chlorophyll** in green plants traps sunlight and uses it to convert **carbon dioxide** and water into **carbohydrates** (energy) for plant growth; and **oxygen**, which it releases into the air.

Sunshine shines on the plant.

The plant takes in carbon dioxide gas from the air.

Green parts of the plant (mostly the leaves) contain chlorophyll.

The plant releases oxygen gas into the air.

Water rises from the soil up through the plant.

physical change   noun

When materials are changed by being heated, cooled, **dissolved** or **evaporated**, the changes are often just physical. This means that the original materials are still there, but in a different form or state.

For example, when water is **evaporated** by being boiled, it looks different, but it is still water.

When it cools it **condenses** back into liquid water. Evaporation and condensation are physical changes: there has been no **chemical change** to the water.

See also: **chemical change**, **reversible change**.

physics   noun

Physics is the study of energy (including heat, light, sound, electricity, magnetism), forces and matter. A scientist who studies these things is called a physicist.

pigment   noun

Pigments are substances that give things colour. For example, skin and hair colour are caused by pigments in the body.

pipette   noun

A pipette is an instrument for measuring small amounts of liquid.

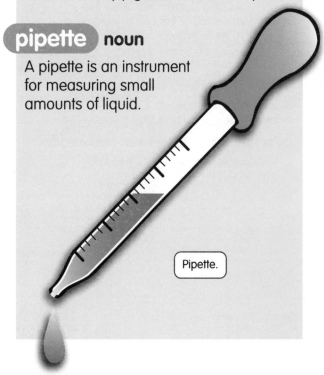

Pipette.

pitch noun

The pitch of a musical note indicates how high or low it is.

Sound is caused by vibrations (to and fro movements), and pitch depends on the time between the vibrations (or their **frequency**). The more frequent the vibrations, the higher the pitch.

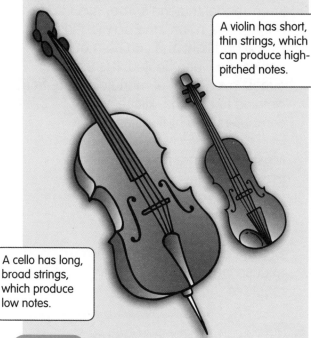

A violin has short, thin strings, which can produce high-pitched notes.

A cello has long, broad strings, which produce low notes.

pivot noun

See **fulcrum** and **lever**.

placenta noun

The placenta is a special organ that develops in and is attached to the **womb** of pregnant, female **mammals**. It regulates the supply of food and oxygen to the developing baby via the **umbilical cord**.

plane noun

Something with an **aerodynamic** shape, such as a wing, is a plane.

planet noun

A planet is a large body of material (solid, liquid or dense gas) that **orbits** a star such as the Sun.

See also: **Solar System**.

plankton plural noun

Plankton are **microscopic organisms** (plant or animal) that float in the sea or in fresh water in very large numbers. They are food for many fish and other sea creatures.

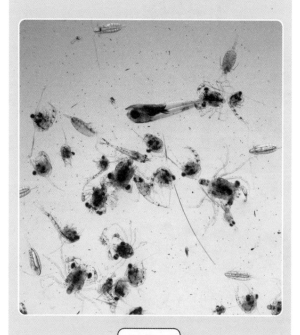

Plankton.

P

plant noun

Plants are living things (or organisms) that grow in soil, on rock or in water. They cannot move about, as some animals can. Plants vary in size from huge trees down to tiny shoots that we can hardly see.

There are several main groups of plants: algae, mosses and liverworts, ferns, and seed plants. Some seed-bearing plants are coniferous (they grow cones); others are flowering plants.

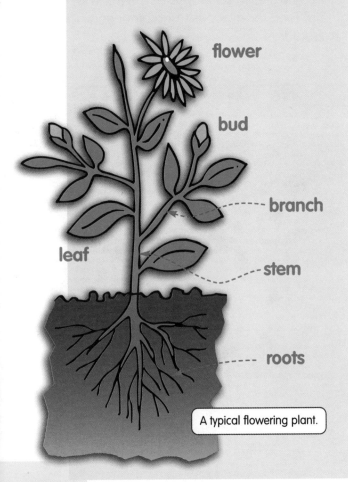

flower

bud

branch

leaf

stem

roots

A typical flowering plant.

plaque noun

Plaque is a layer of material that can form on teeth, if they are not cleaned after eating. Plaque encourages bacteria, which can cause tooth decay.

plastic noun

Plastics are a large group of synthetic (man-made) materials. They include vinyl, polystyrene, nylon, and acrylic. Plastic is strong and light and can be moulded into shape when heated. It is used in almost every form of manufacturing, from clothing to building, kitchenware, computers and hi-fi systems.

Most plastics are now made from petroleum (oil). Plastics are good insulators and are usually not biodegradable.

plastic adjective This word is also used to describe a material which can be moulded.

pneumatic adjective

Objects that are filled with air, for instance tyres, are described as pneumatic. So are machines driven by compressed air: for instance a pneumatic drill.

pole noun

The opposite ends of certain objects, such as **magnets**, are called poles. The Earth's **axis** has a pole at each end; the North Pole and the South Pole. The poles of a magnet are also called north and south, to mark the difference between them.

See also: **magnet**.

pollen plural noun

Pollen are the tiny grains that are produced by the male part of a flower (**stamen**), and carried to the female part of the same or a different flower. This process is called **pollination**. Without pollination, a flower cannot produce seeds.

Hay fever is caused by an **allergy** to pollen.

This is a magnified photograph of the sort of pollen grain that can cause hay fever.

pollination noun

Pollination is the transfer of **pollen** from the male part (**stamen**) of a flower to the female part of that same flower (self-pollination) or another flower (cross-pollination). In cross-pollination the pollen is transported by wind or water; or by birds or insects that visit the flowers. The pollen sticks to them and rubs off on to another flower.

See also: **fertilization**, **reproduction**.

Bee gathering pollen from one plant.

Pollen sticks to bee's legs.

Bee depositing pollen on another plant.

Cross-pollination.

P

pollute verb

Air, water and soil can be polluted (damaged/spoilt) by chemicals or waste products from homes and factories, motor vehicles and chemical **fertilizers** used in farming. The effect of this damage is called **pollution**.

polystyrene noun

A synthetic (man-made) plastic material, often produced as a white, very light foam, used in packaging to protect fragile or valuable objects.

polythene noun

A synthetic (man-made) plastic material used for making fabrics, coverings, and containers. 'Plastic bags' are made of polythene.

pooter noun

A small container with a sucking device, used to capture small organisms.

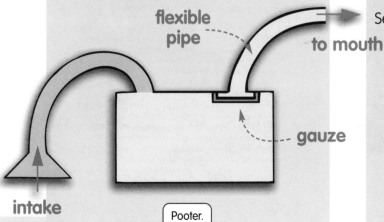

flexible pipe

to mouth

gauze

intake

Pooter.

positive adjective

Electric charge (the amount of electrical energy stored in something) is described either as positive or **negative**. The terminals of a battery (the places to which wires are connected) are also called negative or positive.

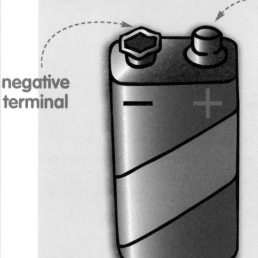

negative terminal

positive terminal

predator noun

A predator is an animal that hunts and feeds on other animals, called **prey**.

predatory adjective Foxes, owls, cats, and humans are all examples of predatory animals.

See also: **food chain**.

prediction noun

A prediction is a statement about something that has not yet happened, but that is expected to happen. Scientists make predictions based on what they have observed in the past; then they carry out tests to see if their predictions are right.

predict verb This means to make a prediction.

I predict that the big parachute will fall more slowly.

Right, we'll test them.

prescription noun

A prescription is a drug that we have been told to take by the doctor. It is also the note from the doctor that allows us to collect the drug from a pharmacist (chemist).

prescribe verb When a doctor tells us to take a medicine, he/she is prescribing it.

pressure noun

Pressure is a **force**. When we press or squeeze something, we put it under pressure, and it pushes back with an equal force. For example, air pumped into a balloon or tyre is under pressure, and this force keeps it inflated.

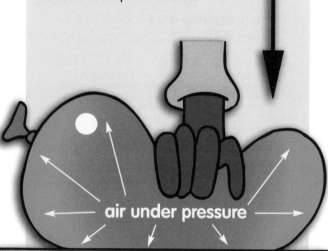

air under pressure

prey noun

Prey means an animal that is hunted and killed by another animal for food.

See also: **predator**.

prism noun

A prism is a transparent, solid shape that can bend rays of light and therefore split white light into the colours of the **spectrum**.

P

process noun

A process is a series of happenings or changes. For example, growing is a process that animals and plants go through. Drying is a process that wet clothes go through when we hang them out.

producer noun

A producer is the first link in a **food chain**. It is often a plant. The producer uses non-living materials such as **minerals** and water, and makes them into food for **consumers** to eat.

consumer

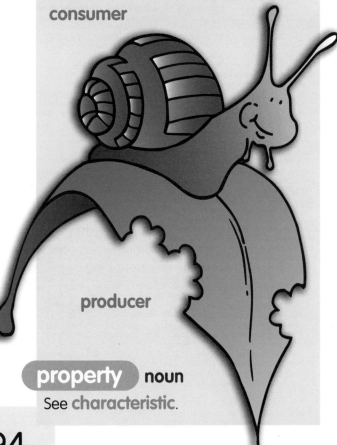

producer

property noun

See **characteristic**.

protein noun

Proteins are an essential part of the human diet; they are needed to provide growth and strength. Foods that contain a lot of protein include eggs, meat, cheese, nuts, seeds, and pulses (for example beans or lentils).

See also: **nutrition**.

puberty noun

Puberty is the stage in the **life cycle** when a child begins **adolescence**. Physical changes occur as the child develops into a sexually-mature person.

pulley noun

A pulley is a simple machine that allows the direction of a pulling **force** to be changed. For example, by pulling down on a pulley, a weight can be raised.

A system of pulleys called a 'block and tackle' can be used to reduce the effort of pulling something, such as a heavy weight.

A simple pulley.

pulse noun

The heart pumps blood around the body with a regular pulse, or beat. The pulse is created by the **arteries** rhythmically expanding as the blood is pushed through them by regular contractions of the heart muscle. The pulse can be felt at several places where an artery is close to the surface, for example at the wrist, temple (either side of the forehead), and neck. The **heartbeat** itself can also be felt in the chest.

pulse rate noun

The number of times the heart beats per minute can be measured by feeling the **pulse** (where an artery passes close to the surface of the skin). This measurement is called the pulse rate. Pulse rates vary from one person to another, from around 45 bpm (beats per minute) up to around 70 bpm. Pulse rate also increases during and after exercise, or with sudden excitement. This is because the heart has to work harder to supply the muscles with oxygen. The pulse rate decreases when we are asleep or when we relax.

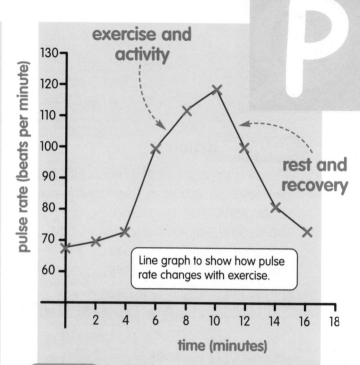

Line graph to show how pulse rate changes with exercise.

pupa noun

During **metamorphosis** many insect **larvae** go through a pupa stage when they are completely inactive. During this stage some wrap themselves in a cocoon of woven hair or leaves. Inside this the pupa makes the amazing change into an adult insect.

Monarch butterfly pupa attached to a leaf.

quadrat noun

This is a square piece of ground (usually 1m^2) that is marked out, so that the range of **organisms** (living things) within it can be studied. Quadrat also refers to the square frame that is placed on the ground to mark out an area.

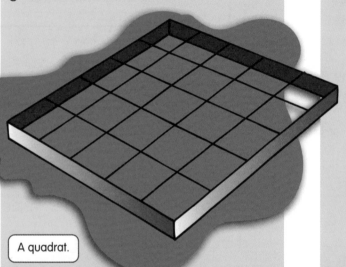

A quadrat.

quarantine noun

A person or animal suspected of having an infectious disease and kept isolated (separate) from others until the danger has passed, is 'in quarantine'.

For example, pets brought from countries where there is **rabies**, spend months in quarantine in case they develop the disease.

quartz noun

This is a hard **crystalline mineral**, found in many of the Earth's rocks. Quartz is one of the minerals that gives **granite** its sparkly look. It is one of the most common minerals on our planet. Most sand consists of grains of quartz.

rabies noun

A dangerous, infectious viral disease that most **warm-blooded** animals can catch. It is passed on in the **saliva** (liquid in the mouth) when an infected animal bites another animal. It affects the **nervous system** and frequently causes death.

radar noun

Radar is a way of detecting the position and speed of moving objects, such as ships and aeroplanes. It works by sending out radio waves, which **reflect** off the object and show on a screen. The word is made from the letters: **RA**dio **D**etection **A**nd **R**anging.

radiation noun

Heat, light and radio waves are examples of radiation. For example, when we feel the warmth of the Sun, we are feeling the effects of heat energy radiating across space.

Some radiation is harmful: for example, ultraviolet rays from the Sun can cause skin **cancer**.

See also: **electromagnetic spectrum**.

radioactive adjective

Some materials, such as plutonium and uranium, are radioactive, meaning that they give off dangerous **radiation**.

ray noun

A ray is a thin or narrow beam of **radiation**: for example, a ray of light.

reaction noun

A reaction is something that happens as a result of something else. For example, if we stretch an elastic band, it **reacts** by pulling in the opposite direction. In science all actions produce some kind of reaction.

Reactions can also take place between different materials. For example when bicarbonate of soda is added to vinegar it reacts by frothing and fizzing as some of the mixture becomes a gas. This is a **chemical change**.

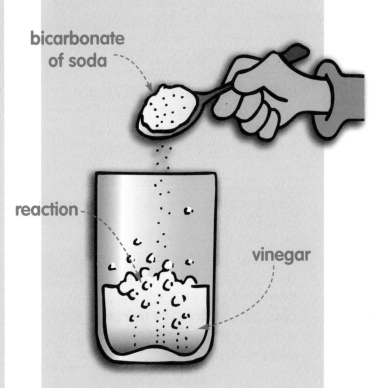

bicarbonate of soda

reaction

vinegar

R

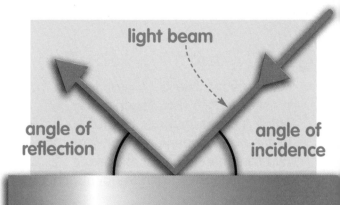

light beam

angle of reflection

angle of incidence

recycle verb

When we recycle materials that have been used, we reuse them to make something new. For example, empty glass bottles from a bottle bank can be melted, and the glass reused.

reflection noun

Reflection is what happens when a **beam** of light strikes a surface. Some of the light is reflected away so that it travels off in a different direction.

We see objects because light reflects from them into our eyes, creating an **image**.

Whatever the angle at which a light beam strikes a flat surface, it is reflected away at the same angle but in the opposite direction. The two angles are called the angle of incidence and the angle of reflection, and they are equal.

refraction noun

When a light beam travels from one material into another, for example from air into a glass of water, or from water into air, it is slightly deflected, meaning it changes direction. This is called refraction.

See also: **lens**.

Light is refracted slightly as it goes from the water into the air, so that a straight straw *looks* bent.

region noun

A region is an area or a certain amount of space. For example, 'the Arctic region', or 'the region around a magnet'.

repel verb

Repel means push away.

repulsion noun A force that pushes things apart is called repulsion (or repulsive force). The opposite is **attraction**.

See also: **magnet**.

reproduction noun

Reproduction is the process by which living things produce new life. There are two main ways of achieving this: sexual reproduction and asexual reproduction. All species need to make new young, so that their species will not become extinct (die out). Humans make young through sexual reproduction. The sperm from a male enters a female body during sexual intercourse (when the **penis** of a male goes into the **vagina** of a female): one of the sperm enters a female egg and fuses (joins) with it. The egg develops into an **embryo** that grows into a baby. Flowering plants also reproduce through sexual reproduction.

See **pollination**.

The process of asexual reproduction occurs in some non-flowering plants and bacteria. Only one parent is needed, and the new plant that grows from the parent plant is identical to it.

reproductive adjective This word is used to describe something connected with reproduction. For example, reproductive organs are the parts of a body or plant used in reproduction.

reptile noun

Reptiles are **cold-blooded** animals with dry, scaly skins. They lay eggs, from which the young are hatched after a period of **incubation** (being kept warm). Reptiles are **vertebrates**. (They have backbones.) Snakes, lizards and crocodiles are all reptiles.

resistance noun

Resistance is a **force** that meets moving objects and slows them down. Air and water both **resist** objects that move through them.

See also: **air-resistance**, **water-resistance**.

Electric **current** (flow of electricity) also meets resistance as it flows around a **circuit**.

See also: **resistor**.

resistor noun

A resistor is any component (part) of an electrical **circuit** that makes the flow of electrical current more difficult. The filament (very thin wire) in a light bulb is a resistor, because it takes more energy than the rest of the circuit to force the current through. This extra energy heats the wire up and makes it glow.

R

respiration noun

All living things respire (breathe) because they all need oxygen to turn **nutrients** into the energy required for living, growing, and reproducing. Respiration is the process of taking in oxygen and expelling (getting rid of) the waste product of **carbon dioxide**.

respiratory system noun

Different organisms have different respiratory systems, meaning that they have different ways of **respiring**. Humans and many other animals breathe air into the lungs and breathe out the waste gases. Fish have gills to absorb oxygen dissolved in water. Worms and many other creatures 'breathe' through the skin.

See also: **lungs**.

reversible change noun

Materials can be changed, for example, by being mixed, heated, cooled, burned, or dissolved. New or different materials may result. If the change is reversible, the new materials can be changed back into the original ones.

For example, salt water can be made by **dissolving** salt crystals in water. The salt water can then be boiled: the water **evaporates**, leaving solid crystals of salt behind.

Dissolving and evaporating are reversible changes.

See also: **irreversible change**, **physical change**.

rib noun

The ribs are bones attached to the **spine**, which form a protective cage around the heart and lungs: the **rib cage**.

See also: **skeleton**.

rock noun

Rock is the main material out of which the Earth's outer **crust** is formed. There are three main types of rock: **igneous**, **sedimentary** and **metamorphic**.

root noun

A plant has a root, or roots, which grow down into the soil and anchor the plant so that it will not be blown or washed away. The roots also absorb water and **nutrients** from the soil; these are drawn up into the plant through narrow tubes.

Teeth also have roots that anchor them in the bones of the head and jaw, and carry nerves and the blood supply to the tooth.

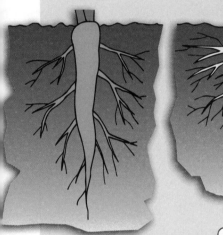

Some plants (e.g. grass or tomatoes) have a tangle of many small roots.

Some plants (e.g. carrots) have a single large tap root, with small branches or hairs coming from it.

rotate verb

To rotate means to turn like a wheel. It takes the Earth 24 hours to rotate on its axis.

R

saliva noun

Saliva is a liquid produced by **glands** in the mouth. It **lubricates** chewed food, so that it becomes easy to swallow, and starts the process of **digestion**.

sandstone noun

Sandstone is a **sedimentary** rock, composed of grains of sand that have become cemented together into a hard, solid material.

Weathered sandstone.

satellite noun

Satellites are objects that orbit (go round) a planet. The Moon is a satellite of the Earth.

The Moon is a natural satellite, but there are also many artificial (man-made) satellites orbiting the Earth. Some are weather observation satellites; some are television and radio satellites that send and receive signals to and from different parts of the world.

saturated solution noun

A solution is a liquid in which another material (called a **solute**) has dissolved. When no more of the solute will dissolve, the solution is saturated.

An example of a saturated solution is a cup of very sweet tea with undissolved grains of sugar at the bottom. The grains will not dissolve, because the liquid around them is **saturated** with sugar.

science noun

Science is a very old word meaning knowledge. It now means a method for studying the natural world by careful **observation** and the testing of ideas by **experiment**.

The three main branches of science are **physics**, **chemistry** and **biology**.

season noun

A year divides roughly into four seasons: spring, summer, autumn and winter. Seasons change because the Earth's **axis** is tilted, so that either the northern **hemisphere** (top half of the Earth) or the southern hemisphere is nearer the Sun and receives more concentrated rays.

When one hemisphere is tilted towards the Sun it is summer there, and it is winter in the other.

Seasons follow each other in a regular, repeating pattern called a **cycle**.

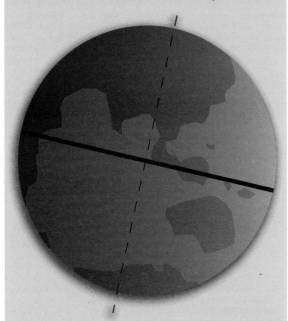

summer - northern hemisphere

winter - southern hemisphere

sediment noun

Sediment means the solid particles that settle to the bottom of a liquid. For example, sand, mud, and animal remains form a sediment at the bottom of lakes and rivers, and on the seabed.

sedimentary rock noun

Sediment is material that has settled at the bottom of rivers, seas, and oceans. At first the sediment is loose, but as it settles into layer upon layer, it is pressed and cemented together into a solid mass. The result is sedimentary rock.

One of the most common sedimentary rocks is **sandstone**.

seed noun

Seeds are the parts of a plant from which new plants grow.

A seed is an ovule (tiny female part of a plant) that has been **fertilized** by pollen. The seeds are dispersed (scattered) by wind or water, or by animals, or by the seed pod bursting open and firing the new seeds away from the parent plant. Other seeds are enclosed inside **fruits**, which fall to the ground and decay, leaving the seed to grow into a new plant.

Seeds **germinate** in the ground, or with water and form **seedlings**, from which new plants grow.

seedling noun

A seedling is a new plant that has started to grow from a seed, after the seed has **germinated** (started to produce a new shoot and root).

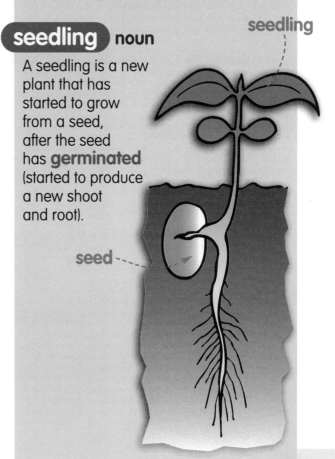

seedling

seed

S

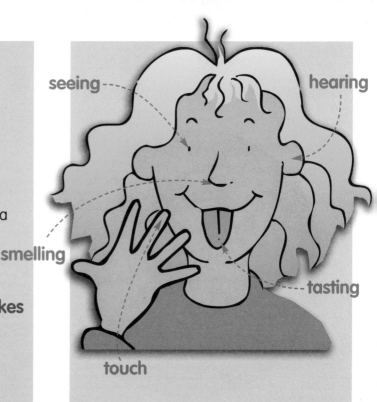

seeing

hearing

smelling

tasting

touch

seismic wave noun

The vibration (shaking) in the ground caused by an **earthquake** is called a seismic wave.

seismology noun

Seismology is the study of **earthquakes** and movements in the Earth's rocky surface.

sense noun

The senses are the means by which living things experience the world around them. Touch, hearing, sight, taste and smell are the senses that humans (and many other animals) have.

sense organ noun

Sense **organs** are the parts of the body with which we see, hear, taste, smell, and touch: in other words the eyes, ears, tongue, nose and skin.

Nerves carry signals from the sense organs to the brain, which processes (deals with) the messages.

sensor noun

A sensor is an electronic device that detects (finds) and/or measures heat, sound, light or pressure.

control

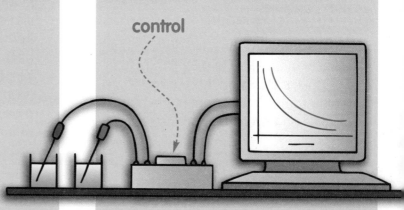

Heat sensors measuring the temperatures of liquids.

sepal · noun

Sepals are leaf-shaped coverings outside the petals of a flower. They protect the flower bud.

sepals

septic · adjective

A wound is septic if it has become infected by **bacteria** and pus (a thick, yellowish substance) has started to form.

sequence · noun

When events follow one after another, this is a sequence.

series circuit · noun

An electrical **circuit** with a single continuous line of wire is a series circuit. If a switch breaks a series circuit at any point, the current stops flowing everywhere in the circuit.

See also: **parallel circuit**.

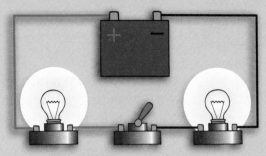

A series circuit.

battery

switch on

sewage · noun

Sewage is the mixture of liquid and solid waste from homes and factories. It is carried by drains (sewers) to sewage works, where it is treated before being returned to the waterways.

shadow · noun

A shadow is a dark outline of an object that forms behind the object when a bright light is directed at it but cannot pass through.

shadow

S

sieve noun and verb

A sieve is a screen or mesh that separates solid particles from a mixture. When we sieve a mixture, only particles smaller than the holes in the mesh pass through.

sink verb

An object sinks when it goes under water or boggy ground. It sinks if it is heavier than water. An object sinks if it weighs more than the same volume of liquid or gas around it.

See also: **buoyant, float**.

skeleton noun

The skeleton is the whole structure of bones that supports the bodies of humans and other animals and protects the vital organs like the heart and brain.

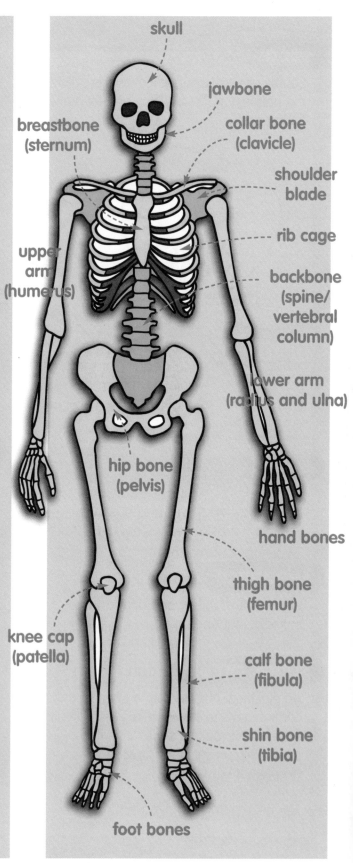

skull

jawbone

breastbone (sternum)

collar bone (clavicle)

shoulder blade

upper arm (humerus)

rib cage

backbone (spine/ vertebral column)

lower arm (radius and ulna)

hip bone (pelvis)

hand bones

thigh bone (femur)

knee cap (patella)

calf bone (fibula)

shin bone (tibia)

foot bones

skull noun

The skull is the bony structure of the head. It surrounds and protects the brain.

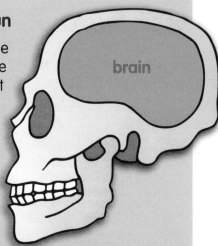

brain

slate noun

Slate is a dark, blue-grey, **metamorphic** rock. It is a good building material, especially for roof tiles, because it is completely impermeable. (Rainwater cannot get through it.)

sodium bicarbonate noun

Sodium bicarbonate (or bicarbonate of soda) is a white, powdery material. When mixed with an acid, such as lemon juice or vinegar, it effervesces (froths) and produces bubbles of **carbon dioxide**.

See **reaction**.

Bicarbonate of soda (mixed with an acid called cream of tartar) is used for baking bread and cakes, because the bubbles make dough 'rise'.

soil noun

Soil is the top layer of the Earth's surface. It is a mixture of small grains of rock and sand, and **humus** (remains of decayed plants and animals). Soils vary from place to place.

For example, some soils contain a lot of **clay**; some are sandy. Soil also changes as we dig further down into the Earth. The different layers of soil form what is called a 'soil profile'.

Soil profile.

solar adjective

Solar means 'to do with the Sun'. For example, a solar **eclipse** is an eclipse of the Sun.

solar cell noun

A solar cell (or solar panel) captures the energy in sunlight and converts it into electric **current**.

Some homes have solar panels on the roof to provide electricity.

solar panels

S

solar power noun

Solar power is energy produced from the Sun's rays. Some homes and factories run on solar power. Small devices, such as calculators, are often solar-powered: they have a cell or panel on them, which turns light into electric **current**.

Satellites orbiting the Earth use the powerful solar **radiation** (energy from the Sun's rays) in space to provide them with the energy they need to function.

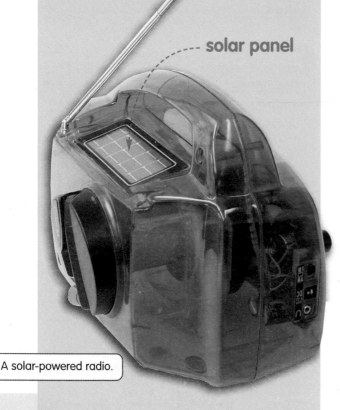

solar panel

A solar-powered radio.

Solar System noun

The Solar System consists of the Sun, the planets and their moons, and the asteroids and comets that orbit the Sun.

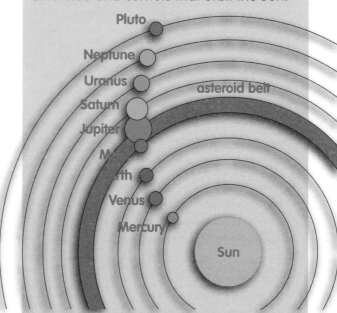

Pluto
Neptune
Uranus
Saturn
Jupiter
Mars
Earth
Venus
Mercury
asteroid belt
Sun

solid adjective and noun

A solid object keeps its shape and does not spread or flow like the other **states of matter** (gases and liquids). Some solids, such as sand and salt, consist of small solid particles or grains. In large numbers these pour like liquids, but each grain is a solid.

Solids change into a liquid state if they are heated up to or beyond their **melting point**.

solidify verb

To solidify means to turn solid or harden. Water solidifies when it freezes and becomes ice at 0 °C. Wet clay solidifies when it dries.

solstice noun

There are two solstices. The summer solstice is the longest day of the year. In the northern hemisphere (the top half of the world) this occurs on 21 June. The winter solstice is on 21 December (the shortest day of the year).

See also: **season**.

soluble adjective

A material that is soluble is one that **dissolves** in a liquid. Salt, for example, is soluble in water.

The opposite of soluble is **insoluble**.

solute noun

A solute is any substance that **dissolves** in another. In a cup of coffee, the coffee granules are the solute.

solution noun

A solution is a liquid in which a solid, gas or other liquid has **dissolved** to form a mixture.

solvent noun

A solvent is a liquid in which another substance **dissolves**.

A liquid that removes stains is also called a solvent, because it dissolves the substance that made the stain.

sonar noun

See **echo**.

sound noun

Sound is made when something **vibrates**, and it can be heard. It is a type of energy, and it travels in **waves**. The vibrations need a medium through which to travel to the **ear**, for example, air. Sound can also travel through liquids and some solids. It cannot travel through a **vacuum**.

Sound travels at about 330 metres per second.

See also: **frequency, pitch**.

species noun

A species is the smallest group into which living things are divided. A tiger, for example, is one species of cat, which is one kind of **mammal**, which is one kind of animal.

See also: **kingdom**.

spectrum noun

A spectrum is a range. The spectrum of visible light, for example, is the range of colours made by the different wavelengths of light.

White light contains the whole spectrum of colours. But **refraction** (bending of light beams) by glass/Perspex or liquid can separate the beams to make bands of different-coloured light. This is what happens when sunlight is refracted by drops of rain in the air, creating a rainbow.

A rainbow effect can also be created by a thick block of glass (or **prism**) or by the surface of a CD, which also scatters light beams into different wavelengths.

sperm noun

Sperm are the microscopic male cells that fertilize the female eggs during animal reproduction.

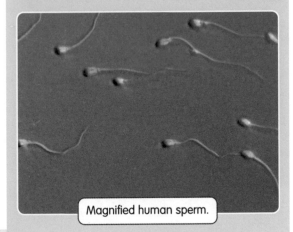

Magnified human sperm.

spine noun

The spine is the backbone in the **skeleton** of humans and many other animals. It consists of a row of bones called **vertebrae**, which are slotted together, with pads of tissue (called cartilage) in between. This forms the vertebral (or spinal) column. The spinal column is hollow in the centre and through it runs the spinal cord (the nerves which connect the brain to other parts of the body).

stalactite noun

Water dripping down from the roof of a limestone cave is rich in dissolved **minerals**, such as **calcium**. Each drip deposits (leaves behind) a tiny amount of these dissolved minerals on the rock, and over years or centuries these can grow down from the roof in a cone-shaped structure, called a stalactite.

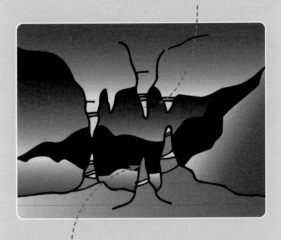

stalactite

stalagmite

stalagmite noun

Stalagmites form on the floor of caves for the same reason as stalactites, except that the minerals are deposited after the drop of water reaches the ground.

stamen noun

The stamen is the male part of a flower that produces **pollen**. It usually consists of a short supporting thread (called the filament) with a blob on the end (called the anther) where the pollen is made and stored before it is used.

See also: **fertilization**, **flower**.

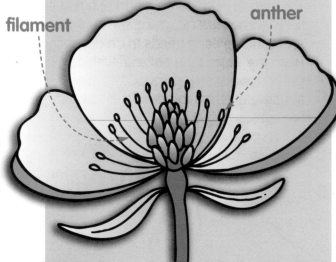

filament

anther

star noun

A star is a massive ball of gas in space, which radiates heat and light due to the burning materials within it and on its surface. The Sun at the centre of our **Solar System** is a star. All the other stars we can see are so far away that they appear as pinpricks of light in the night sky. The nearest star is about 40 thousand billion kilometres from Earth.

The Sun is our nearest star. It provides Earth with heat and light energy.

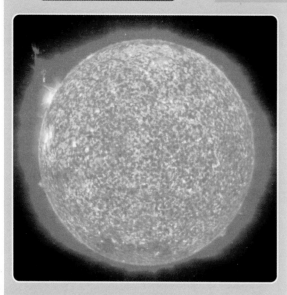

states of matter noun

Materials can be in one of three states: **liquid**, **solid** or **gas**. A material can change from one state into another without becoming a different material. Ice is a solid; water is a liquid; water vapour is a gas, but all three are made of the same combination of **elements**: oxygen and hydrogen.

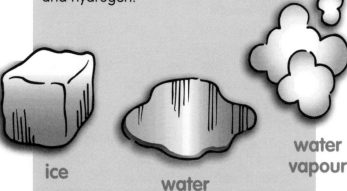

ice

water

water vapour

The changing states of matter.

111

S

static electricity noun

Static electricity is a charge that builds up in an object that is surrounded by an **insulator**, such as air. It is usually caused by rubbing or **friction**. If the object is touched or approached by a **conductor**, the electricity discharges. If it is a very powerful charge, it can make a spark. **Lightning** is a discharge (a release) of electricity from a charged cloud.

If we touch something, or someone, charged with static electricity, we can feel a mild electric shock, and sometimes hear the discharge as a sharp crackling sound.

stem noun

The main body of a plant from which the leaves and flowers grow is the stem.

sterilize verb

When we clean something with a disinfectant or with very hot water, we sterilize it. This kills any germs that might be on or in it. Surgical instruments have to be sterilized before use.

Sterilizing also means operating on an animal (a pet, for instance) so that it cannot reproduce (have young).

stethoscope noun

A stethoscope is an instrument that doctors use to listen to a patient's breathing and heartbeat. It consists of a hollow disk connected by tubes to earpieces.

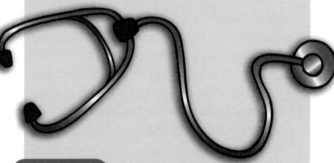

stigma noun

The stigma is the female part of a flower on which **pollen** (carrying male reproductive cells) needs to be deposited. From the stigma the pollen develops a pollen tube, which grows down along the style and into the **ovary** to fertilize the ovules (eggs).

See also: **flower**.

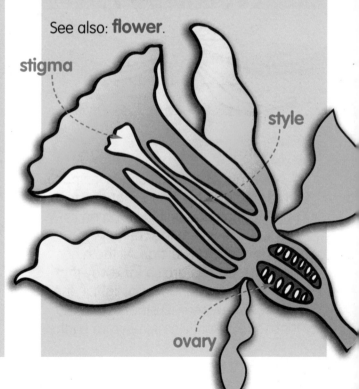

stigma

style

ovary

stomach noun

The stomach is at the base of the **oesophagus** (the tube which carries food from the mouth to the stomach). In the stomach digestive juices (including **acid**) are mixed in with the food and start to break it down into **nutrients** that the body can use. From the stomach the food moves into the small **intestine**, to continue the digestive process.

streamlined adjective

Something that is shaped to travel quickly and easily through air or water is streamlined. An arrow is streamlined; so is a rocket. Many birds and fish have streamlined bodies, for swimming and/or flying.

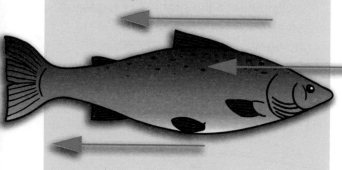

A fish has a sharp nose and thin fins for cutting through water.

style noun

The part of a flower that connects the **ovary** to the **stigma** is called the style.

See also: **flower**, **stigma**.

sun noun

A sun is a **star**. The Sun (the star at the centre of our **Solar System**) is a massive ball of burning (or reacting) gases. It is very large: over 100 times the diameter of the Earth, and it is around 140 million kilometres away.

On account of its great mass, the Sun exerts strong gravitational forces, which hold planets, asteroids and comets in orbit around it; the Earth is one of the planets.

The heat and light from the Sun provide the energy that enables plants and animals to live and grow. However, the Sun also sends out some dangerous radiation (energy). Too much exposure to the Sun can cause skin **cancers**. It is also very dangerous to look directly at the Sun: blindness can result.

sunrise noun

Sunrise is the appearance of the Sun over the eastern **horizon** each day. The Sun does not really rise: it appears to because the Earth rotates (goes round).

See also: **sunset**, **axis**.

sunset noun

Sunset is the disappearance of the Sun below the western **horizon** each evening.

See also: **sunrise**.

S

S

sunspot noun

Sometimes there are violent disturbances on the surface of the Sun. They appear as darker patches, and are called sunspots. They occur in a regular **cycle** of about 11 years; it is thought that they are caused by strong magnetic forces on the Sun.

Warning! It is very dangerous to look directly at the Sun: sunspots should only be looked at on photographs.

supersonic adjective

Sound travels through air at around 1200 km per hour near ground level, but higher up in the atmosphere it travels more slowly. Travel that is faster than the speed of sound is described as supersonic. Aircraft, like Concorde, which fly faster than sound, are also described as supersonic.

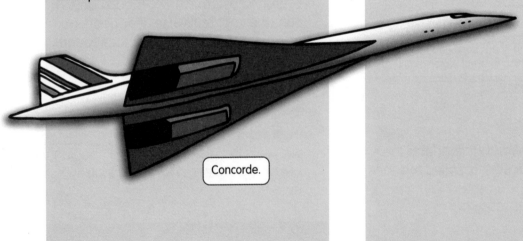

Concorde.

switch noun

A switch is a device that makes a temporary break in an electric circuit, so that current stops flowing.

A switch is described as 'open' when the circuit is broken and the current is 'switched off'. When the switch is 'closed' the circuit is reconnected, and the current is 'switched on'.

symbiosis noun

Symbiosis takes place when two different species live together and help each other. For example, **micro-organisms** live in the intestines of humans. They benefit from living in a warm place, but also benefit the human (their host) by assisting with the process of digestion, so that the body can absorb the nutrients. There is a **symbiotic relationship** between the micro-organisms and the human.

teeth plural noun

Teeth are hard, bone-like objects that are rooted in the head and jaw of many animals. Teeth have a soft core covered by a hard layer of material called dentine. This is coated with enamel, which protects the tooth.

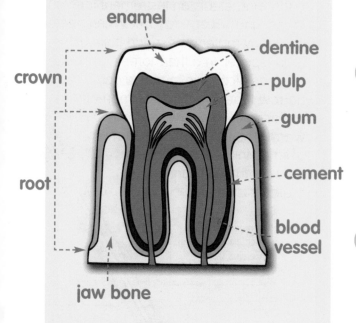

enamel
dentine
crown
pulp
gum
root
cement
blood vessel
jaw bone

Teeth vary in shape according to their function. Incisors are teeth which cut food: they have a straight, sharp edge, like a chisel. Canine teeth are for tearing food: they are pointed. Molars are for chewing or grinding food: they have a flat top, called a crown.

Teeth also vary from animal to animal, depending on the food the animal eats. A shark, for instance, has rows of sharp pointed teeth, with which it rips its prey.

telescope noun

Telescopes are instruments for looking at distant objects on Earth or out in space.

Telescopes use lenses and/or mirrors to gather light and magnify images.

See also: observatory.

temperature noun

Temperature is a measure of how hot or cold something is. It is given in degrees. The standard unit is degrees Celsius, written °C. Zero °C is the temperature at which water freezes; 100 °C is the temperature at which water boils.

tendon noun

Tendons are bands of tough body tissue that connect muscles to the bones.

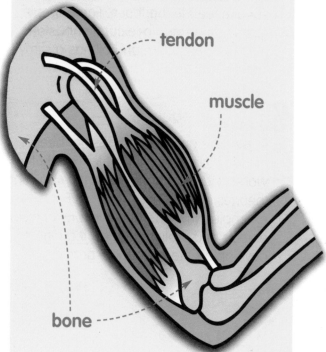

tendon
muscle
bone

T

terminal noun

See negative and positive.

testicle noun

Testicles are the male organs that produce sperm (reproductive cells).

See also: reproduction.

textiles plural noun

Textiles are fabrics made by weaving or knitting; or any of the fibres and yarns used in making fabrics.

texture noun

The texture of a material is the way its surface feels to the touch. For example, glass has a smooth texture; sandstone has a rough texture and oil has a slimy texture.

theory noun

A theory is an idea that has not been proven. Scientists attempt to explain the world and what happens in it by building theories based on evidence. For example, Newton's observations of falling objects and orbiting planets led him to develop his theories about gravity.

thermal adjective

Thermal means to do with heat. A thermal conductor, for example, is a material that conducts heat well.

thermometer noun

A thermometer is an instrument for measuring temperature. When heated up, many materials expand (take up more space). In a thermometer a liquid (such as alcohol) expands along a very narrow tube when the thermometer is placed in or near something warm. The length of the column of liquid in the tube shows how hot the surrounding material is.

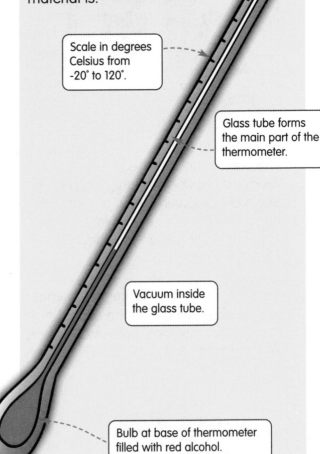

Scale in degrees Celsius from -20° to 120°.

Glass tube forms the main part of the thermometer.

Vacuum inside the glass tube.

Bulb at base of thermometer filled with red alcohol.

thermostat noun

A thermostat is a device with a heat sensor that responds to a change of temperature in some way. For example, a thermostat in a room may switch off the heating when the air temperature reaches a certain point; a thermostat in a car engine activates a cooling fan if the engine becomes too hot.

thorax noun

The thorax is the part of a human body that is also called the chest.

In an insect the thorax is the middle of the three body sections. The others are the head and the abdomen.

thunder noun

See lightning.

tide noun

Tides are the regular rising and falling of sea level, which can be seen around the coastline. Tides are caused by the force of gravity between the Earth, Moon and Sun.

tobacco noun

Tobacco is a plant. Its dried leaves are smoked as a drug.

tooth noun

See teeth.

toxic adjective

Toxic means poisonous. Toxic waste is poisonous waste.

toxin noun

Toxin means poison, or any material that can cause disease or harm.

translucent adjective

A material that is translucent allows light to pass through it. Translucent materials are not necessarily transparent. Frosted glass is translucent, but we cannot see images clearly through it.

transparent adjective

A transparent material, such as glass or clean water, allows light to pass through it and images to be seen clearly through it.

transpiration noun

Transpiration takes place when water or other liquid passes out through the pores (tiny holes) in the leaves of plants.

Transpiration is part of the water cycle. For example, water in the soil is taken up by plants and transpired by the leaves. It joins with the water vapour in the air and eventually returns to the soil as rain.

T

trilobite noun

Trilobites were sea creatures that lived in water 570 million years ago. At that time shallow seas covered many places that have since become dry land. Trilobites grew up to 18 centimetres in length, and were the largest animals of their time. They had feathery legs, and feelers which they used to find food.

Only fossils of trilobites remain.

A fossil trilobite (actual size).

tumour noun

A tumour is an abnormal growth on or inside the body. Some tumours are not harmful, and stay in one place; these are called benign tumours. Others, which are malignant or cancerous, grow rapidly and spread and can cause illness and even death.

turbine noun

A turbine is a machine in which one part called a rotor turns when a force (such as wind, or fast-moving water, or the pressure of steam) is exerted on it. The turning movement of the turbine can be converted, by means of magnets, into electrical energy.

See also: hydroelectric power.

ultraviolet adjective

See electromagnetic spectrum.

umbilical cord noun

The umbilical cord joins a foetus (or unborn baby) to the placenta in the mother's womb. The placenta supplies the foetus with nourishment and removes waste products from it. When the baby is born, the umbilical cord is cut and knotted to form the navel (or 'belly-button').

universe noun

The whole of space, together with the planets, stars and galaxies, make up the universe.

upthrust noun

The upward force that a fluid (liquid or gas) exerts on an object that is placed in it or on it is called upthrust. If upthrust is greater than the weight of the object, the object floats upwards or stays on the surface.

Upthrust is really the result of downward forces. The weight of an object sinking down into a fluid, such as water, forces the water level to rise. It is the weight of this water pushing back that causes upthrust on the object.

See also: buoyant.

Upthrust keeps the duck afloat.

urine noun

Waste products are removed from the blood by the kidneys and passed out of the body as a yellow liquid called urine.

uterus noun

See womb.

vaccine noun

Vaccines contain germs of a particular disease that have been killed or weakened. When these are injected into a person or animal, the body produces **proteins** (called antibodies) which are capable of fighting the real disease. Someone who has been vaccinated in this way becomes **immune** to the disease for some time afterwards.

Vaccination was invented in 1796 by an English doctor named Edward Jenner, who discovered that infecting somebody with the mild disease of cowpox made him or her immune to the more serious disease of smallpox.

Successful vaccines have since been produced for many diseases, including polio, measles, and diphtheria.

Injecting a vaccine is also called **inoculation**.

vacuum noun

A vacuum is a space in which there is no matter. If we pump all the air out of a container, we create a vacuum inside it.

A **vacuum flask** has hollow sides which have been emptied of air and sealed. A vacuum is a very good **insulator**: it prevents heat loss, and so can keep liquids hot; it also prevents heat gain, and can therefore keep liquids cool.

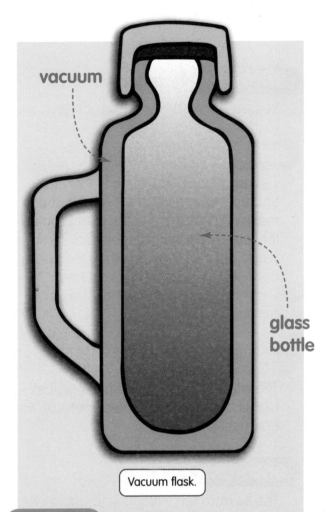

vacuum

glass bottle

Vacuum flask.

vagina noun

The vagina is the opening and passage to the **womb** in female mammals.

valve noun

A valve is a device in the heart and in **veins** that allows blood to flow in one direction only.

vapour noun

A gas-like substance, such as mist or steam, that is formed when a liquid is heated.

See also: **condense**, **states of matter**.

vegetable noun

Vegetables are edible plants or parts of plants: leaves, roots, flowers, fruit, seeds.

Cabbage, for example, is a leaf; broccoli and cauliflower are flowers, carrots are roots. Some of the foods we call vegetables are really the **fruit** of a plant: for example, cucumbers, marrows, and tomatoes.

vegetation noun

Vegetation means any plant life: for example, trees, bushes, and grasses.

Some regions are covered in vegetation. Others, like rocky islands, are almost bare of vegetation.

vein noun

Veins are **blood vessels** (tubes in the body) through which the blood travels back to the heart, after being pumped to the muscles and organs of the body.

Veins are visible, for example in the wrist, as blue lines under the skin. There is no **pulse** in a vein, because the blood is just draining back to the heart, not pumping, as it does in the **arteries**.

See also: **circulatory system**.

velocity noun

Velocity means speed in a particular direction.

vertebrate noun

A vertebrate is an animal with a spinal column, or backbone. Birds, mammals, reptiles, amphibians and fish are all vertebrates.

vibrate verb

When something moves rapidly backwards and forwards, or up and down, it vibrates.

Sound is caused by **vibration**. For example, a vibrating guitar string sends sound-waves to the small drum inside the ear, making it vibrate. These vibrations are sensed by the brain as sound.

See also: **ear**.

V

virus noun

viral adjective

Viruses are tiny **parasites** (organisms that live on another organism). They invade the body's cells and cause **viral** diseases.

Millions of people throughout the world suffer each year from viral diseases such as AIDS, polio, measles, chicken pox, mumps, flu and the common cold. Viruses also produce illnesses such as foot-and-mouth disease in animals.

Viruses are extremely small and can only be seen with an **electron microscope**. Outside a living cell, a virus is dormant (or sleeping) and can remain like that in body fluids. Once inside a cell, however, the virus becomes active and can produce thousands of new viruses.

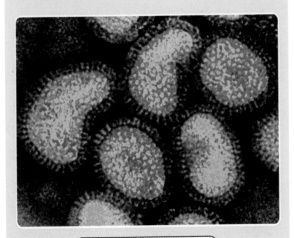

Magnified influenza virus.

viscous adjective

viscosity noun

A viscous liquid is one which is thick and pours or flows slowly.

vitamin noun

Vitamins are materials that are found naturally, for example in plants and fish oils, and which we need in small doses to remain healthy. For example Vitamin C is found in fresh fruit and vegetables and is essential for healthy cells and body organs.

volcanic adjective

Materials that come from a volcano, or events caused by volcanoes, are described as volcanic: for example, volcanic ash, volcanic **lava**, a volcanic eruption.

volcano noun

A volcano is a break or opening in the Earth's **crust** from which molten **lava** and gases pour. This pouring out is called an eruption. As the lava spills out and then cools, the volcano grows into a tall, cone-shaped mountain.

A volcano is described as active when it is erupting. At other times it is dormant (sleeping). Dormant volcanoes can 'awaken' and erupt again, sometimes after centuries of being dormant.

Volcanoes (like **earthquakes**) occur where there are weaknesses or faults in the Earth's crust, for example around the coastlines of the Pacific Ocean. This area has a large number of active and dormant volcanoes, which is why this region is often called the Ring of Fire.

Voltage measurements are given on batteries. A typical torch battery is 1.5 volts. Voltage can be increased by connecting two or more batteries in series (in a row).

Molten lava flowing from an erupting volcano in Hawaii, 1983.

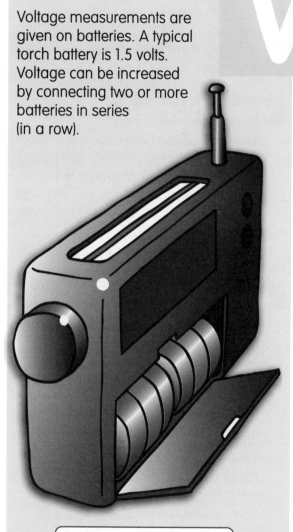

Two batteries connected in series.

voltage noun

The difference in electric charge (amount of electricity) between two points (for example, the two terminals on a battery) is called voltage and is measured in **volts**. It is the difference in charge that causes an electric **current** to flow when the two points are connected to form a **circuit**.

volume noun

Volume is the amount or quantity of something, and it can be measured. For example, the volume of water in a school pond can be measured in litres. The volume of the space inside a box or room can be measured and given in cubic metres or cubic centimetres.

Volume is also used to describe the loudness of sound, and is measured in decibels.

warm-blooded adjective

Animals that use heat energy from food to control body temperature are described as warm-blooded, for example humans and horses. They are different from **cold-blooded** animals, whose body temperature varies according to their surroundings.

water noun

Water is a **compound** (mixture) of hydrogen and oxygen. At normal temperatures it is a liquid, but it can freeze into solid ice; and it can boil or evaporate to become **water vapour**.

Water **dissolves** many materials, including salt and other **minerals**. Dissolved minerals make seawater salty.

Water is one of the most commonly found substances on planet Earth. It fills the seas, rivers and oceans, and falls from the sky as rain. It is essential for life, and all animal bodies and plants contain a large proportion of water.

water cycle noun

In the water cycle, water on the Earth's surface **evaporates** into the air, where it **condenses** into clouds and falls back to the earth as rain or snow. Then the cycle starts all over again.

water resistance noun

Friction between water and an object moving through it is a force that slows the object down and makes it harder to move, especially at high speed.

Water resistance is reduced when the shape of the moving object is **streamlined**.

See also: **air resistance**.

water vapour noun

When water **evaporates** (dries up) it changes into a colourless gas called water vapour. Water in an open container evaporates slowly from the surface. If water is heated to **boiling point**, however, bubbles of vapour (or steam) form and the water is converted from a liquid to a gas more quickly.

When water vapour or steam cools, it **condenses** back into liquid drops of water.

The white colour that we see in steam and clouds and mist is tiny droplets of water that have begun to condense from the vapour.

Water freezes at 0 °C and boils at 100 °C.

waterproof adjective

A material that is waterproof does not absorb water or let water pass through it. Glass, most plastics, rubber, and roof slates are all waterproof.

Cotton, paper, leather, and bare wood are not waterproof; they are absorbent.

watt noun

Watts are a unit for measuring power: for example, the power needed to run a motor or light a bulb.

Light bulbs have their **wattage** written on them. Normal house lights use either 60 or 100 watts, but energy-saving bulbs need a lot less; they save money and conserve energy.

wave noun

A wave is a movement or disturbance in air or water and other materials, that travels away from its source (where it started). For example, if a pebble is dropped into calm water, waves spread out in rings.

Vibrations send waves through the air, which we hear as sound. Light and other radiation (energy) also travels in waves.

Waves have peaks and troughs (highs and lows). The distance from one peak to the next is called the **wavelength**. Different types of waves have different wavelengths. Some have short wavelengths (for example X-rays) and some have long wavelengths (for example radio waves).

See also: **electromagnetic spectrum**.

The number of waves that are sent, for example in a second, is the 'frequency' of the wave. The height of the wave (which is the amount of disturbance it causes) is called its 'amplitude'.

In a sound wave the amplitude is what makes the sound loud or quiet; the frequency is what makes it high or low. (See **pitch**.)

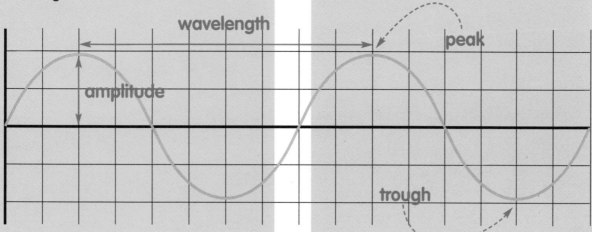

weight noun

Weight is a **force**. Objects have weight because they are pulled downwards towards the Earth by the force of **gravity**.

Weight can be measured in **newtons** on a **force meter**.

The more **mass** an object has, the more it weighs. However, in science, 'weight' and 'mass' do not mean the same.

See also: **mass**.

womb noun

The womb (also known as the uterus) is the pear-shaped organ situated in the pelvic (hip) area in women and other mammals in which the **foetus** (unborn baby) develops.

X-ray noun

X-rays are high-energy invisible light beams that can pass through some solids. They are used to take X-ray photographs of the inside of a person's body to see, for example, if a bone is broken.

See also: **electromagnetic spectrum**.

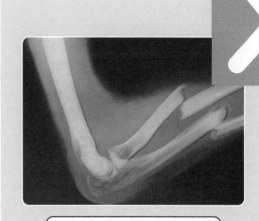

Coloured X-ray of a broken arm.

yeast noun

Yeast is a type of **fungus** that produces **carbon dioxide** gas. Yeast is used in bread making because the bubbles of carbon dioxide make the dough rise, or swell up. Yeast in fruit juices causes them to **ferment**, producing carbon dioxide and **alcohol**. It is used in wine and beer making.

Magnified yeast cells.

zoology noun

Zoology is the study of anything in the animal kingdom.

See also: botany.

Acknowledgements

The authors and publisher would like to thank the following for permission to reproduce photographs:

Corbis

Page 35 Grant Smith; 57 Bettman

Dorling Kindersley Images

Page 5 Barrie Watts; 58; 67; 89

Doug Smith

Page 5; 29; 32; 39; 43; 47; 59; 63; 71; 72; 77; 108

Jef Barrett

Page 12

Science Photo Library

Page 4 Jeremy Walker; 11 Andrew Syred; 14 Rosenfeld Images Ltd; 18 Tom McHugh; 22 Simon Fraser; 23 Jerry Lodriguss; 33 Martin Dohrn; 38 Edelmann; 40 Martin Land; 49 European Southern Observatory; 50 Dr Gary Gaugler; 63 Dr Jeremy Burgess; 66 Kent Wood; 69 Gusto; 73 David Parker; 74 Dr Tony Brain; 75 Jerry Schad; 81 David Parker; 91 David Scharf; 95 John Mitchell; 110 Pascal Goetgheluck; 111 European Space Agency; 122 Dr Linda Stannard, UCT; 123 Soames Summerhays; 127 Dept of Clinical Radiology, Salisbury District Hospital; 127 David Scharf